THE ME FACTOR
Your Secret Weapon for Author Visibility

THE ME FACTOR

Your Secret Weapon for Author Visibility

LISA TOWLES

INDIES UNITED
PUBLISHING HOUSE, LLC

Published April 2026
by Indies United Publishing House, LLC

Cover Art by Tatiana Fernandez

FIRST EDITION

ISBN: 978-1-64456-888-0 [Paperback]
ISBN: 978-1-64456-889-7 [Kindle]
ISBN: 978-1-64456-890-3 [ePub]

Library of Congress Control Number: 2026905060

INDIES UNITED PUBLISHING HOUSE, LLC
P.O. BOX 3071
QUINCY, IL 62305-3071
INDIESUNITED.NET

Praise for The ME Factor

"This is not a book of shortcuts or performative marketing tactics. Towles has created a system that helps authors understand who they are, what they offer, and why that matters. The ME Factor concept is disarmingly simple and profoundly clarifying: it gives authors permission to stop chasing what everyone else is doing and start building visibility from the truth of who they are. That's what sells books. This book is pure gold!"

Leo Bottary, Founder of Peernovation and Author of *Peernovation 365*

"In The ME Factor, Lisa Towles codifies her experience as an award-winning crime novelist and corporate communications executive to establish one's own authenticity and voice as the bedrock on which authors can build their enduring brand. Her framework shows how authors can connect very intentionally with readers through an emotional promise that keeps them coming back to YOU again and again."

Craig Pinegar, *Enterprise Technology Investment Leader*

"The ME Factor is a bit of marketing magic, clearly written and easily explained with excellent examples, ideas, and help to get you on track and keep you there. The best book on marketing I've read."

Ana Manwaring, Author of *Mortal Revenge* and *Kickback*

"Thoughtful, exacting, and quietly radical; a redefinition of what it means to be visible as an author."

The Prairies Book Review

"Visibility isn't luck. It's positioning. The ME Factor clearly defines strategy authors can actually use so they stop blending in and start being chosen."

Jane Ubell-Meyer, Founder, *Bedside Reading*

"I'd always been proud of hitting #1 in my categories, but I hadn't fully internalized what it meant to rank Top 50 in Contemporary Romance and Top 15 in Romantic Suspense—without running paid Amazon ads. Seeing that in context reframed how I think about my audience, my reach, and how I talk about my work. It wasn't just a nice moment—it was *evidence*."

Nikki Davenport, Author of *International Incident*

"A mix of hard-nosed strategy and real empathy... Towles treats the author as the CEO of a small but serious brand. *The ME Factor* turns book marketing from a foggy mystery into a clear plan."

Literary Titan

"Until now, no one has created an end-to-end process for creating a successful book using contemporary marketing communications. Lisa Towles, a well-known author of 14 popular thrillers, has applied her authorial expertise and business acumen to develop a comprehensive success guide for both fiction and non-fiction writers."

Eric C. Wentworth, Author of
A Mindful Career* and *A Plan for Life

For Lee

Your courage, creativity and spirit are a constant inspiration.

True love makes everything possible.

ALSO BY LISA TOWLES

Specimen
Codex
Terror Bay
The Ridders
Switch
Salt Island
Hot House
Ninety-Five
The Unseen
Choke

And Published Under the Name Lisa Polisar

Escape: Dark Mystery Tales
The Ghost of Mary Prairie
Blackwater Tango
Knee Deep

"There is only one you. And there will never be another one. That's your power."

— Mel Robbins, The 5 Second Rule

Table of Contents

INTRODUCTION: CONTEXT & CONFIDENCE
PART I: THE HEART – Your Identity
- Chapter 1: The Soul of the Strategic Author
- Chapter 2: The ME Factor – Your Unfair Advantage
- Chapter 3: The Emotional Promise – What Readers Come Back For

PART II: THE INTELLIGENCE – Finding Your Place in the Market
- Chapter 4: Market Intelligence – Know Where You Fit
- Chapter 5: Audience Insights & Reader Personas
- Chapter 6: Market Gaps – Find Your White Space

PART III: THE STRATEGY – Building Your Author Brand
- Chapter 7: Author Branding – Where It All Comes Together
- Chapter 8: Content Pillars – Your Strategic Messaging
- Chapter 9: Brand Expression – Showing Up Consistently

PART IV: DIAGNOSTICS – What's Working (and What's Not)
- Chapter 10: SWOT – Your Secret Edge
- Chapter 11: Platform Check – Know Your Power

PART V: DIGITAL VISIBILITY – Find Your Readers
- Chapter 12: Content That Works
- Chapter 13: Social Media with Soul
- Chapter 14: Crack the Amazon Code

PART VI: HUMAN CONNECTION – Beyond the Screen
- Chapter 15: Human Connection – Marketing's Missing Link

- Chapter 16: Beyond the Page – Your Visibility Multipliers
- Chapter 17: Self-Care --A Competitive Advantage

PART VII: LONGEVITY – The 90-Day Rhythm
  - Chapter 18 – Stay Sharp, Stay Strategic

CONCLUSION: DIFFERENTIATION AS A DISCIPLINE

GLOSSARY
ABOUT THE AUTHOR
ACKNOWLEDGEMENTS
AUTHOR SUPPORT

INTRODUCTION
CONTEXT & CONFIDENCE

An estimated four million new book titles enter the global market every year.

Four million.

That number should feel impossible—and yet, it's real. Traditional publishers, hybrid presses, and self-published authors are all competing for the same readers, the same shelf space, the same fleeting moment of attention in an endless scroll.

And you're entering it—or trying to survive in it—with a book you've poured months or years into creating. Whether you're a seasoned executive writing your first book on leadership or a novelist launching your fifth thriller, the challenge is the same: how do you stand out when the market is this saturated?

The instinct, when confronted with this reality, is often

paralysis or panic. Some authors freeze, waiting for the right moment or right platform. Others throw themselves into frantic activity—posting everywhere, trying every tactic, running ads—hoping sheer volume of effort will break through.

Sometimes this works, but not consistently.

In this landscape, visibility requires three things: knowledge, positioning, and intent.

You need to understand who you are as an author, where you fit competitively, who your readers are, and how to reach them deliberately. Without this foundation, even dedicated, hardworking authors can spend years doing the right things—building websites, posting consistently, pitching bookstores—and still struggle to gain traction.

Not because the tactics are wrong, but because there's no connective tissue holding them together. Without a strategic framework, your efforts scatter. The website says one thing, your social media profiles say another, and the book positioning feels disconnected from both. The individual pieces might be good, but they're not creating a cohesive brand.

This book gives you the framework. Once you have that foundation, everything you do has a place to anchor. The wires connect.

You already think strategically.

If you've built a career in business, the frameworks in this book—Market Intelligence, SWOT Analysis, Brand Positioning—will feel familiar. They're adapted from the same strategy tools you've used in boardrooms. The difference is application: instead of positioning a product, you're positioning yourself. The thinking is the same. The context is new.

If you're a writer, you solve strategic problems every day. You evaluate character motivations, assess whether a subplot serves the narrative, decide which scenes to cut. You make a million structural decisions about pacing and emotional impact. That's strategic thinking—you just might not call it that.

This book gives you frameworks to organize the strategic tools and instincts you already have. You're not starting from zero.

What you've been missing isn't capability. It's a system.

You've been handed conflicting advice from every direction: Build a platform. Be authentic. Post three times a day. Run ads. Grow organically. Be on TikTok. Write to market. Write what you love.

All of this advice might be valid for someone, somewhere—but without a framework, you have no way to know what's right for YOU. So you either try everything (and burn out), do nothing (and stay invisible), or pick tactics randomly and wonder why they don't work.

This book gives you the system.

A way to understand your identity, assess your market, build your brand, diagnose your position, and execute with clarity. Not because you need to do everything, but because you need to do the right things—the things that align with who you are, where you fit, and the readers you serve.

The ME Factor isn't about reinvention. It's about clarity. It's about protecting your creative work with the same strategic thinking you'd apply to any valuable asset. It's about building visibility that's grounded in truth: who you are, what you offer, and why readers who need your stories will be able to find them.

Here's something you need to hear before we go any further: **This system gives you permission to be yourself.**

Your actual personality. Your quirks. Your wry humor or

intensity. The way you talk, not the way you think an "author" should sound. These aren't obstacles to overcome in your marketing. They're not unprofessional or inappropriate or too much or not enough. Those unique aspects are your competitive advantage.

In a market where so many books compete for attention, manufactured personas don't break through. Generic "author voices" blend together. But you—the actual you, with your specific perspective and energy and way of seeing the world—are unrepeatable. When you bring your real self into your book promotion, your social media, your reader engagement, you create something no algorithm can replicate and no competitor can copy: genuine human connection.

This book will give you strategic frameworks—the ME Factor, Market Intelligence, Brand Pillars. But strategy doesn't mean performance. It means understanding yourself clearly enough to show up authentically, consistently, and in the places where your real readers are waiting for you.

You don't need to become someone else to succeed. You need to become comfortable with revealing yourself.

You can do this. Not because it's easy, but because you already have the capability. You just need the framework.

What This Book Will Give You

This book isn't a collection of marketing hacks or a 30-day launch checklist. It's a strategic framework for building long-term author visibility in a competitive literary marketplace.

Your *ME Factor* is your positioning tool—the intersection of who you are, where you fit in the market, and who you serve. It's not a logo or a tagline. It's the answer to the question every reader unconsciously asks: "Why should I care about YOUR books instead of the thousands of others like them?" This framework helps you articulate what makes you unmistakable, not just marketable.

This book is structured around five strategic foundations that build on each other:

Identity → You'll define your ME Factor, understand your emotional promise to readers, and establish the "why" behind your work. This isn't fluffy self-discovery—it's the business case for your author career.

Intelligence → You'll learn Market Intelligence strategies to understand your competitive landscape, identify *white space* in your genre, and build accurate reader personas based on data, not assumptions.

Branding → With identity and market knowledge in place, you'll synthesize them into a cohesive author brand—complete with content pillars that make your platform strategy repeatable and maintainable.

Diagnostics → You'll conduct a professional SWOT analysis to assess your strengths, weaknesses, opportunities, and threats. You'll audit your current platform and identify where you need to focus (not where everyone says you "should" be).

Execution → Only then—with strategic clarity—will you execute. You'll learn how to choose platforms strategically, create content that aligns with your brand, optimize your Amazon presence as discovery infrastructure, and conduct outreach that feels authentic rather than desperate.

Throughout the book, you'll also learn **how to calibrate**—how to know if what you're doing is working, which metrics matter for your goals, and when to pivot versus when to persist.

How to Use This Book Based on Where You Are

If you're a debut author: Start at the beginning and work through sequentially. You're building a foundation from scratch, and each section prepares you for the next. Pay special attention to Market Intelligence (Part II) and Reader Personas (Chapter 5)—understanding the landscape before you enter it gives you a strategic advantage most debut authors don't have.

If you're a returning author: Skim Part I (you likely know your identity), then dive deep into Part II (Market Intelligence) to understand what's changed since you last published. The digital landscape has shifted dramatically—Parts V and VI will catch you up on platform strategy and visibility tactics that work now.

If you're mid-career but stuck: Jump directly to Part IV (Diagnostics). Conduct your SWOT analysis to understand why you've plateaued, then work backward through Parts I-III to identify misalignments between your identity, market position, and brand expression. Often, stagnation comes from brand drift —you've evolved but your platform hasn't.

If you're a business executive writing your first book: You'll recognize the strategic frameworks immediately—they're adapted from business strategy tools you've likely used. Focus on Part II (Market Intelligence) and Part III (Branding) to translate your business thinking into publishing context. The execution chapters (Parts V-VI) will feel more tactical, but they're grounded in the strategy you've already built.

Why This Isn't Just Another Marketing Book

Most author marketing books start with tactics: set up social media, run ads, build a website. They assume you already know who you are, who your readers are, and how you fit in the market. When those tactics don't work, authors blame themselves—or worse, they assume they need to work harder, post more, spend more.

This book starts with strategy: Identity first. Market

understanding second. Brand clarity third. Only then do tactics make sense. This approach respects both the creative and business sides of your author career. You won't be asked to become someone you're not, perform authenticity you don't feel, or chase every trending platform. You'll build a system that's grounded in who you are and what your readers need.

The frameworks in this book are the same ones I use in my consulting practice—and the same ones I apply to my own author career. They're tested, practical, and designed for authors who think strategically about building careers, not just launching books.

By the end, you'll have clarity about your positioning, confidence in your decisions, and a repeatable system for visibility that doesn't require you to be everywhere or do everything.

Your creative work deserves intentional positioning.

Let's build that together.

What Inspired Me to Write This Book

I bridge two worlds that rarely intersect: high-level business strategy and the lived experience of being a working author.

Over 18 years in corporate communications, I built my career translating complex business objectives into narratives that drove market differentiation and revenue results. I've worked across communications, marketing, and customer experience—always with the same goal: aligning brand strategy to external stakeholders in ways that create measurable impact. I hold an MBA in IT Management and multiple certifications in different sub-areas of digital marketing and AI implementation. I've also served as Board President of an award-winning nonprofit, leading strategic planning, stakeholder engagement, and mission-driven growth. Strategy isn't just what I teach—it's what I've practiced in boardrooms, product launches, and organizational leadership at the highest level.

But I'm also a crime novelist with 14 published books. In 20 years of writing, I've navigated every corner of the publishing industry: small presses, academic publishers, hybrid models, traditional deals, and self-publishing. I've launched books that succeeded and books that didn't. I've built platforms from scratch, pivoted when algorithms changed, and learned—often the hard way—what moves the needle for author careers. My most recent thriller, *Switch*, published in 2025, reflects two decades of evolution as both a storyteller and a strategist.

Most consultants come from one side or the other—business experts who don't write, or writers with no corporate experience. I live in both spaces daily, understanding creative vulnerability and business discipline equally.

This dual perspective is what drives my Story Impact Consulting practice. I don't just teach frameworks—I've tested them in my own career. The Market Intelligence tools in this book – I use them to position my own releases. The SWOT analysis process - I run it as an author every six months. The brand pillars are how I turned scattered social media presence into focused community building that converts to readers and long-term fans.

I founded Story Impact Consulting because I kept watching talented authors make the same strategic mistakes—not from lack of effort but lack of business thinking applied to creative work. They were drowning in tactics (post daily, run ads, be on every platform) without the strategic foundation to make smart decisions about where to focus their limited time and resources —and losing sight of perhaps the most important ingredient: WHY they write, why their stories matter, and why readers should care.

My approach is outcomes-driven and collaboration-based. I ask authors the questions that reveal their "why," help them see their books as long-term career assets rather than one-off projects, and ensure their voice and vision align with the readers who will become their advocates. I've worked with debut authors finding their footing, mid-career authors navigating plateaus, and business professionals writing their first books who bring strategic thinking but need publishing fluency.

Communication is my gift. Marketing is my talent. Strategy is my superpower.

Whether you implement the frameworks in this book independently or decide you want a strategic partner to accelerate the process, my goal is the same: to support you by giving you clarity, confidence, and a repeatable system for building visibility that doesn't require you to become someone you're not.

Your story deserves strategic protection. Let's make sure it gets heard above all the noise.

PART I

THE HEART: YOUR IDENTITY

Before seeking an audience, an author must define the "emotional fingerprint" of their work. This section establishes the author as the CEO of their creative brand.

If you're writing or marketing your first book: This section establishes the foundational clarity most authors skip—defining who you are as an author, what makes you different, and what emotional experience readers can count on from your work.

If you've published but struggle to gain traction: This section reveals why generic positioning fails and shows you how to articulate what makes you distinct in a crowded market—the difference between being one of thousands and being the only one who does what you do.

If you're returning to publishing after a long break: Use this section to reassess your positioning. What's changed in your work, your goals, and how you want to show up? This gives you permission to evolve rather than recreate what no longer fits.

CHAPTER 1

THE SOUL OF THE STRATEGIC AUTHOR

Strategy is not a four-letter word.

It sounds corporate. Calculating. Like you're supposed to engineer authenticity or manufacture connection. It feels like the opposite of why you started writing in the first place—to tell stories, to explore ideas, to create something meaningful.

But here's what most authors don't realize: strategy isn't the opposite of creativity. It protects it.

Strategy gives your book legs—enough to reach your target readers.

Strategy is what ensures your creative work reaches the readers who need it. It's what prevents you from burning out, scattering your energy, or giving up after years of effort. Strategy isn't about becoming someone you're not. It's about being intentional with who you already are.

This chapter bridges the gap between the creative spark that drives your writing and the professional path that sustains your author career. Because you can't build a career on inspiration alone—and you shouldn't have to choose between artistic integrity and strategic thinking.

WHAT: Strategic Thinking for Authors

Strategic thinking is the practice of making intentional decisions based on understanding where you are, where you want to go, and what resources you have to get there.

For authors, this means:

Knowing your identity. Who you are as an author, what makes your work distinct, and what readers can consistently expect from you. This isn't branding in the superficial sense— it's self-knowledge applied to your creative output.

Understanding your market. Where you fit in the competitive landscape, who your readers are, and what gaps or opportunities exist. This isn't "selling out"—it's recognizing that even the most literary, artistic work exists in a context with other books competing for the same readers' attention and money.

Making informed decisions. Choosing which book to write next, which platforms to invest time in, where to allocate your limited budget, and when to pivot versus when to persist.

Strategic authors don't guess. They assess, decide, and act with clarity.

Building realistic systems. Creating repeatable processes for writing, marketing, and connecting with readers that don't require constant reinvention or burnout-level effort. Strategy creates leverage—the ability to do less but accomplish more because your efforts are aligned and connecting with your purpose.

Strategic thinking doesn't mean you plan every move years in advance or that you never take creative risks. It means you make decisions consciously rather than reactively. You understand the "why" behind your choices. You can articulate your positioning. You know what success looks like for you— not according to someone else's definition—and you're building toward it intentionally.

Let's establish something critical: **Strategic thinking doesn't mean manufactured thinking.**

When business executives hear "brand strategy" or "market positioning," they sometimes assume it requires adopting a persona—a polished, professional version of themselves that fits a template. When creative authors hear the same terms, they often fear they'll have to become someone they're not: extroverted when they're introverted, salesy when they hate selling, constantly "on" when they need solitude to create.

Neither assumption is true.

Strategic thinking means understanding who you are, where you fit, and how to communicate that clearly. It means making decisions based on your real strengths, your real readers, and your real capacity—not on what you imagine you should be doing.

The authors who build real visibility aren't the ones who contort themselves into someone else's model of success. They're the ones who get clear about their own identity and build systems that honor it. Strategic doesn't mean fake. It means intentional.

Here's what strategic thinking is NOT:

It's not manipulation. You're not tricking readers or manufacturing false authenticity. You're communicating clearly about who you are and what you offer.

It's not rigid planning. Strategy adapts. Markets shift, readers evolve, and you grow as a writer. Strategic thinking includes the flexibility to pivot when data suggests a different path.

It's not "selling out." Writing to market and writing what you love aren't mutually exclusive. Strategy helps you find the intersection—the place where your authentic creative vision meets genuine reader demand.

It's not just for business books or nonfiction. Literary fiction, poetry, experimental work—all benefit from strategic thinking about positioning, audience, and visibility. Art that no one sees doesn't fulfill its purpose.

The authors who thrive long-term aren't just the most talented writers. They're the ones who combine craft with strategic thinking. They understand that creating great work is only half the equation—the other half is ensuring that work finds its audience.

WHY: Why This Matters for Creative Professionals

You might be thinking: "I just want to write. Why do I need to think like a business strategist?"

Because the publishing landscape has fundamentally changed —and not in ways that favor passive hope or organic discovery. But here's the encouraging truth: strategic thinking levels the playing field. You don't need a massive publisher, a huge marketing budget, or insider connections. You need clarity about who you are, who you serve, and how to reach them intentionally.

The market reality:

With so many new titles entering the market annually, traditional gatekeepers (agents, publishers, reviewers) can't possibly evaluate or champion every worthy book. Algorithms determine visibility on retail platforms. Social media platforms change their rules constantly, making organic reach nearly impossible without paid promotion. Readers are overwhelmed by choices and rely on signals—covers, reviews, recommendations, author platforms—to filter their options.

The Data: Research shows that brands prioritizing quality over quantity see engagement surge by nearly 20%, even as posting frequency decreases. The difference isn't posting more often—it's being more intentional about what you post.

In this environment, talent alone isn't enough. The world is full of brilliant writers whose books languish in obscurity—not because the work isn't good, but because no one knows it exists. Not because they didn't try to promote it, but because they promoted it without strategy, scattering effort across tactics that didn't align with their goals or their readers' behavior.

This is why strategy matters: it's advocacy for your work.

When you think strategically about your author career, you're not abandoning your creative principles. You're ensuring those principles reach the people who will be moved by them. You're respecting your work enough to give it the best possible chance of success. You're taking responsibility for your career rather than hoping someone else—an agent, a publisher, an algorithm—will do it for you.

Strategy is what separates authors who build careers from authors who write books.

Consider two authors who both write literary thrillers:

Author A writes a brilliant debut. Gets some early reviews. Posts sporadically on social media when they remember. Has a basic website that hasn't been updated in two years. Doesn't have a clear sense of who their ideal reader is or where those readers congregate. Launches their second book with the same scattered approach. Sales plateau. They don't understand why—the second book is even better than the first.

Author B writes a brilliant debut. Before launch, they study comparable titles to understand positioning. They identify where their ideal readers spend time (book clubs, specific subreddits, certain podcasts). They build a simple email list and a focused social presence on two platforms where their readers are. They create content pillars aligned with their brand that feel natural, not performative. They approach bookstores with a clear pitch about who they serve. When they launch their second book, they have a system—repeatable, sustainable, effective. Sales grow.

Same quality of writing. Different outcomes. The difference isn't talent—it's strategy.

Author A works just as hard as Author B. They post on social media. They do book events. They spend money on ads. But they're pushing pins without a framework—their efforts don't stick because there's no connective tissue connecting them.

Author B isn't more talented. They're more intentional. They made decisions based on understanding their positioning, their audience, and their resources. They built a system that expands over time rather than starting from scratch with each book.

For business executives writing their first book:

You already understand this. You've built strategies, positioned products, and allocated resources under constraint in your professional life. You know that good products don't sell themselves—they need positioning, messaging, and go-to-market plans. Your book is no different. The strategic thinking you've honed in boardrooms applies directly here. The challenge isn't learning to think strategically—it's applying that thinking to a new context where the metrics, channels, and audience behaviors are unfamiliar.

For writers without business backgrounds:

You might feel like strategic thinking is foreign territory. But you already do this in your writing. Every time you plot a novel, you're thinking strategically about structure, pacing, and emotional payoff. Every time you revise, you're making resource allocation decisions—what to cut, what to expand, where to focus your limited time. Every time you study books you admire, you're conducting competitive analysis. The language might be different, but the thinking is the same.

The cost of not thinking strategically:

Burnout. You try everything, exhaust yourself, and see minimal return on your effort.

Invisibility. Your books exist, but readers can't find them in the noise.

Financial loss. You spend money on tactics (ads, services, tools) without understanding if they're right for your goals.

Creative stagnation. You write the next book without understanding why the last one didn't connect, so you repeat the same strategic mistakes.

Career abandonment. After years of effort without results, you stop writing altogether—not because you lack talent, and not because you don't enjoy it, but because the demands feel too draining.

The benefit of thinking strategically:

Clarity. You know who you are, who you serve, and how to reach them.

Efficiency. Your efforts align rather than scatter.

Sustainability. You build systems that work without constant hustle.

Growth. Each book builds on the last because you understand what's working and why.

Creative freedom. Strategy creates the space and resources for you to keep writing—because your career is financially and emotionally sustainable.

This isn't about choosing between art and commerce. It's about ensuring your art has a fighting chance in a crowded, noisy, algorithm-driven market. Strategy is how you honor your creative work by giving it the visibility it deserves.

HOW: Shifting from Reactive to Strategic Mindset

The shift from reactive to strategic thinking isn't a personality transplant. It's a series of small mindset tweaks that change how you make decisions about your author career.

Reactive thinking asks: "What should I do right now?"

Strategic thinking asks: "What outcome am I trying to create, and what's the most effective path to get there?"

Reactive thinking says: "Everyone says I need to be on TikTok."

Strategic thinking asks: "Where are my actual readers, and am I strong in that format?"

Reactive thinking responds: "Sales are down—I need to run more ads."

Strategic thinking diagnoses: "Why are sales down? Is it positioning, audience mismatch, market saturation, or something else? What's the root cause, not just the symptom?"

Here's how to make the shift:

1. Start with "Why" Before "What"

Before you take any action—launching a book, starting a newsletter, running ads, posting on social media—ask yourself: "What am I trying to accomplish, and why does this tactic serve that goal?"

Most authors reverse this. They hear advice ("You need to post daily on Instagram") and implement it without asking if it aligns with their goals or audience. They're busy, but not effective.

Strategic authors start with the goal, then choose tactics that serve it.

Example:

Reactive: "I should start a TikTok account because BookTok is a massive community of readers."

Strategic: "My goal is to grow my email list with readers who love dark psychological thrillers. My readers are typically 35-55, professional women. Is TikTok where they discover books? Let me research. If not, where ARE they? Facebook? Book clubs? Goodreads? I'll focus there instead."

2. Prioritize Based on ROI, Not Noise

You can't do everything. You have limited time, energy, and budget. Strategic thinking means ruthlessly prioritizing based on what will give you the greatest return on investment (ROI) —not what's trending or what other authors are doing.

Ask: "Of all the things I could do, which will move me closest to my goal with the resources I have?"

Reactive authors try to be everywhere. They post on five social platforms, run ads on three channels, attend every event, and burn out within six months.

Strategic authors choose two platforms where their readers are, build systems that make content creation easy, and focus effort where it will bring back real value.

3. Build Systems, Not One-Off Efforts

Reactive authors reinvent the wheel with every book launch. They scramble to create content, reach out to reviewers, figure out their messaging—all from scratch, every time. If that's you, first – you're remarkable. You're doing something incredibly difficult without a roadmap. The shift from reactive to strategic is just about organizing what you're already doing.

Strategic authors build repeatable systems. They have:

- A launch checklist that's refined with each book
- Content pillars that make social media manageable
- A media kit that's updated rather than recreated
- A network of reviewers and bookstores they've cultivated over time
- Email templates for outreach that are proven to work

Systems create leverage. The second book launch is easier than the first. The third is easier than the second. You're leveraging prior work rather than resetting to zero every time.

4. Make Decisions Based on Data, Not Feelings

Feelings matter—but they're not always the most reliable guides for strategic decisions.

You might *feel* like your book isn't resonating. But what do your reviews actually say? Are readers praising your voice but struggling with pacing? Are they loving the characters but confused by the plot? Data tells you where to focus your development.

You might *feel* like Instagram isn't working. But what's your engagement rate? Are you gaining the right followers (your readers) or random follows? Is your content aligned with your brand pillars, or are you posting randomly?

Reactive authors make decisions based on anxiety or comparison. "That author has 50,000 followers—I must be doing something wrong."

Strategic authors make decisions based on their own data and goals. "My email list is small but highly engaged. My open rate is 35% (well above industry average). I'm reaching the right people—I just need more of them. I'll focus on list growth, not follower count."

5. Embrace "Good Enough" Over Perfect

Strategic thinking includes knowing when to stop optimizing and start executing.

Perfectionism is often a disguise for fear. You keep tweaking your website, refining your book description, or searching for the "perfect" social media strategy—but you never actually launch because nothing feels ready.

Strategic authors understand that done is better than perfect.

They launch, gather data, and iterate based on what they learn. Version 1.0 doesn't need to be flawless—it needs to exist so you can improve it to Version 2.0.

6. Think in Experiments, Not Failures

When something doesn't work—a book doesn't sell, an ad campaign flops, a social platform doesn't gain traction— reactive authors spiral. "I'm terrible at marketing. Nothing works. I can't do this."

Strategic authors reframe. "That was an experiment. What did I learn? What would I do differently next time?"

Every book launch, every campaign, every tactic is a test. Some will work better than others. The goal isn't perfection— it's learning, adjusting, and improving over time.

CALIBRATION: Signs You're Thinking Strategically vs. Just Busy

How do you know if you're thinking strategically—or just exhausting yourself with activity that looks productive but isn't moving you forward?

Here are the diagnostic questions:

"Just Busy" Indicators:

✖ **You're exhausted but not seeing results.**

You post every day, run ads, attend events—but your email list isn't growing, sales are flat, and you feel like you're shouting into the void. Activity without strategy is just noise.

✗ You can't explain your positioning.

Someone asks, "What kind of books do you write?" and you ramble for three minutes without clarity. Or you say, "I write thrillers," but so do 100,000 other authors. What makes YOU distinct?

✗ You chase trends reactively.

"BookTok is hot—I need to be there!" But you haven't asked: Is this where *my* readers are? Am I strong in short-form video? Does this align with my brand? You're chasing noise, not opportunity.

✗ You make decisions based on comparison.

"That author has 1M followers—I must be failing." You don't know their engagement rate, whether those followers convert to readers, or if their goals are the same as yours. Comparison without context is anxiety, not strategy.

✗ Every book launch feels like starting over.

You haven't built systems, so each launch requires the same scramble: create content, find reviewers, figure out messaging. You're working hard but not building leverage.

✗ You can't measure what's working.

You don't track email growth, engagement rates, conversion from social to sales, or which platforms drive readers. You're guessing, not assessing.

Strategic Thinking Indicators:

✔ **You can articulate your positioning in one sentence.**

"I write dark psychological thrillers for readers who love unreliable narrators and moral ambiguity."

"I write epic fantasy for readers drawn to immersive worlds where magic and destiny shape impossible choices."

"I write wellness books for overwhelmed professionals who need science-backed strategies they can actually implement in 15 minutes a day."

If you can clearly state who you are and who you serve, you're thinking strategically. You have clarity about your identity and audience.

✔ **You know why you're doing what you're doing.**

When someone asks, "Why are you on Instagram?" you don't say, "Because everyone says I should be." You say, "Because my ideal readers are visual-focused women 35-50 who discover books through aesthetic posts and author connection. My engagement data shows this is working."

✔ **You can trace effort to outcomes.**

You don't just post on social media and hope. You track: Does this platform grow my email list? Do my followers really buy books? Are they the right readers (enthusiastic, engaged) or just random follows?

Strategic authors measure what matters and adjust based on

data.

✓ **You prioritize based on goals, not guilt.**

You don't attend every author event, respond to every opportunity, or chase every trend. You assess: Does this serve my strategic goals? If not, you decline—without guilt.

✓ **You have systems, not scrambles.**

Your book launches aren't panic-inducing. You have a repeatable process. Your content creation doesn't require daily reinvention—you work from pillars. Your outreach isn't improvised—you have templates and relationships.

✓ **Your efforts evoke ROI.**

Each book builds on the last. Your email list grows steadily. Your relationships with bookstores deepen. Your brand recognition strengthens. You're not starting from zero with every project.

The Calibration Exercise:

Ask yourself these questions honestly:

1. **Can I clearly state who I am as an author and who I serve?**

2. *(If no → Chapters 2-3 will help you define your identity and positioning)*

3. **Do I know where my ideal readers discover books?**

4. *(If no → Chapters 4-7 walk you through Market*

Intelligence and reader research)

5. **Can I explain why I'm on the platforms I'm on?**

6. *(If no → Chapters 13-14 will help you audit your platform strategy)*

7. **Am I tracking any metrics, or just "trying things"?**

8. *(If not tracking → Chapters 11 and 18 teaches you what to measure and when)*

9. **Do I have repeatable systems, or do I reinvent everything each time?** *(If reinventing → Chapters 9-10 show you how to build smart systems)*

10. **Are my efforts moving the needle, or do I feel like I'm stuck in place?**

11. *(If stuck → Chapter 10 (SWOT) will help you diagnose why)*

If you answered "no" to most of these, you're busy—but not strategic. And that's okay. This book will teach you every single one of these skills. Strategy can be learned. You don't need an MBA or a marketing background. You just need to move from scattered effort to focused intention. The chapters ahead give you the frameworks, step by step.

WORKROOM: Your Strategic Foundation

You're already thinking strategically. You're juggling creativity and business, showing up for readers, learning as you go. This 20-minute exercise captures that thinking and turns it into a decision-making tool you can use throughout this book—and throughout your career.

Here's what makes the Workroom sections valuable: Every

chapter in this book will give you frameworks (ME Factor, SWOT, Reader Personas, Content Pillars). But frameworks only work when they're applied to *your* specific situation. The Workroom exercises do that work. They translate general strategy into your personal roadmap.

This first exercise builds your strategic foundation. The answers you document here will:

- Guide which frameworks matter most for *your* goals (Chapter 2's ME Factor, Chapter 10's SWOT)
- Help you prioritize what to focus on when you reach the execution chapters (Parts V-VI)
- Give you a baseline to measure against during your quarterly reviews (Chapter 18)
- Create clarity that makes every subsequent decision easier

Think of this as calibrating your compass before the journey. Twenty minutes now, and every chapter that follows becomes more personally relevant.

1. What does success look like for my author career?

Not what you think you "should" want. Not what other authors have. What do YOU want?

- A full-time income from writing?
- Critical acclaim and literary recognition?
- A passionate community of readers who love your work?
- Creative freedom to write what you want without financial pressure?

Write it down. Be specific.

2. What am I currently doing that feels misaligned with that goal?

Are you chasing follower count when what you really want is deep reader connection? Are you writing to trends when you want creative freedom? Where's the disconnect between your actions and your actual goals?

3. If I could only focus on THREE things this year to move my author career forward, what would they be?

Not ten things. Three. Strategic thinking is about prioritization. What are the highest-leverage activities that serve your specific goals?

4. What's one system I could build that would make my author life easier?

A launch checklist? Email templates for bookstore outreach? Content pillars for social media? Pick one system to build this month.

Strategic thinking isn't about becoming someone you're not. It's about being intentional with who you already are. It's about ensuring your creative work—the stories, ideas, and perspectives that matter to you—reach the people who need them.

You already think strategically as a writer. Now you're applying that same thinking to your career.

You've got the strategic mindset. Next up – discovering what makes you unmistakable.

CHAPTER 2

THE ME FACTOR: YOUR UNFAIR ADVANTAGE

You are not your genre.

If you've ever felt like your author bio sounds like everyone else's, you're not alone. "Award-winning author of contemporary fiction..." "Passionate storyteller exploring the human condition..." "Writer of page-turning thrillers that keep you up at night..."

These aren't bad descriptions. They're just not you. They're generic placeholders that could describe thousands of authors. They don't answer the question every reader unconsciously asks when discovering a new author: "Why should I care about YOUR books instead of the hundreds of others competing for my attention?"

Introducing…your ME Factor.

The ME Factor isn't your tagline, your logo, or your color palette. It's the authentic intersection of who you are, what you offer, and who you serve. It's your positioning—the clear, specific answer to what makes you distinct in a crowded market. Not just marketable. Unmistakable.

This chapter helps you discover and articulate your ME Factor using a simple formula: Goal + Audience + YOU. By the end, you'll be able to introduce yourself with clarity and confidence —identifying and reframing what was already there.

WHAT: The ME Factor Concept

The ME Factor is your unique positioning as an author—the specific combination of your creative identity, your market position, and the readers you serve.

It answers three essential questions:

1. What do I want to accomplish with my writing? (Your Goal)

Not just "write books" or "get published"—but what kind of impact, income, or legacy you're building toward. Your goal shapes everything else.

2. Who am I writing for? (Your Audience)

Not "everyone who likes thrillers" but a specific reader with specific needs, preferences, and emotional triggers. The clearer your audience, the clearer your positioning.

3. What do I uniquely bring to my work? (YOU)

Your voice, your perspective, your expertise, your themes, your emotional signature. The elements that make your books feel distinctly yours—even if a reader couldn't see your name on the cover. Your "YOU" is your brand positioning and your authentic self.

The ME Factor Formula:

Goal + Audience + YOU = Your ME Factor

When these three elements align, you have positioning. You know who you are, who you serve, and why readers should choose your books over the alternatives.

Your ME Factor Components

GOAL + AUDIENCE + YOU = BRAND POSITIONING

What the ME Factor is NOT:

It's not a persona you create for marketing purposes. You're not inventing a character or "playing author." The ME Factor isn't about reinvention—it's about recognition. What makes you unmistakable already exists. You're identifying and articulating what's already authentic about your work, not manufacturing something for public consumption.

It's not restrictive. Your ME Factor doesn't lock you into writing the same book forever. It's flexible enough to evolve as you grow, but clear enough that readers know what to expect from you. When you have a clear ME Factor, you gain more creative freedom—because your readers trust you, not just your genre.

It's not about being the "best." You don't need to be the most talented writer in your genre. You need to be the most YOU. The authors who build successful careers aren't necessarily the most gifted—they're the most clearly positioned. They've stopped apologizing for what makes them different and started leveraging it. Yes, showing up feels vulnerable until you realize: the things you're self-conscious about (your speaking voice, how you look on camera, your quirks) are often exactly what makes you memorable to the right readers.

It's not your genre alone. "I write mystery" isn't a ME Factor. So do many other authors. Your ME Factor is what makes YOUR mysteries different—the perspective, themes, voice, or expertise that only you bring.

The power of this framework isn't that it helps you become someone marketable. It's that it gives you permission to be strategically yourself. To stop trying to fit into someone else's template of what an author "should" be. When you know your ME Factor, every decision becomes simpler. You know which platforms to say no to. Which opportunities aren't worth your energy. Which partnerships align with who you are and which ones would require you to perform.

Your ME Factor is your filter, your compass, and your competitive advantage, when you're willing to honor the truth of who you are.

Examples of ME Factor Positioning:

Fiction:

Weak: "I write romance novels." Strong: "I write second-chance romance for readers who want complicated characters and messy, earned happy endings—not instant fairy tales."

Weak: "I'm a thriller author." Strong: "I write corporate espionage thrillers for readers who want insider authenticity and morally gray protagonists navigating power and betrayal."

Nonfiction:

Weak: "I write business books." Strong: "I write for burned-out mid-career managers seeking practical frameworks to reclaim agency in toxic work cultures—from someone who's navigated corporate politics for 20 years."

Weak: "I'm a leadership expert." Strong: "I help first-time executives build inclusive leadership cultures through evidence-based practices, not trendy buzzwords—for leaders who want repeatable results."

See the difference? The strong versions give specificity, showing which kinds of stories or frameworks, who they're for, and what makes them distinct.

WHY: Differentiation Matters in Crowded Markets

With so many new books entering the literary market every year, being *good* isn't enough. Neither is *talented* or *great* if no one knows what makes you different.

Readers don't discover books randomly anymore. They discover them through algorithms, recommendations, and social proof—all of which require clarity about positioning. If you can't articulate what makes you distinct, algorithms can't surface you to the right readers, bookstores can't pitch you effectively, and readers can't explain to their friends why they should read your work.

The Data: Books with specific, differentiated positioning see 20% revenue increases compared to generically positioned books in the same genre. When readers know exactly what they're getting, they buy with confidence.

Differentiation isn't about being weird or gimmicky. It's about being specific. It's about owning what makes your work recognizable—so readers who love what you do can find you quickly, and readers who don't can move on without wasting time.

Why Generic Positioning Fails

When you position yourself generically "I write business books"), you're competing with everyone. Every business author becomes your competitor. Readers have no way to distinguish you from the noise.

When you position yourself specifically ("I write claustrophobic psychological thrillers set in isolated academic settings, exploring the cost of ambition"), you've narrowed your competition dramatically. You're not competing with everyone—you're competing with the small subset of authors who write similar content. And readers who love that specific subgenre will find you irresistible.

Generic positioning creates comparison fatigue. Readers look at your book and think, "This looks like every other thriller book. Why should I pick this one?"

Specific positioning creates recognition and desire. Readers think, "This is exactly the kind of book I've been looking for."

For Business Executives Writing Nonfiction

You understand this instinctively from your corporate experience. A strong brand delivers a consistent promise—Volvo promises safety, Apple promises innovation, Patagonia promises environmental responsibility. Customers return because they trust that promise will be kept.

Your author brand works the same way. If your first book promised "validated and understood," your second book needs to deliver that same emotional core—even if the topics differ.

The executives who successfully build thought leadership platforms aren't necessarily writing about the same topic over and over—they're delivering the same emotional experience repeatedly. Readers trust the feeling they'll get, regardless of the specific subject.

For Fiction Writers Building Careers

You might think, "But I don't want to be pigeonholed. What if I want to write different kinds of books?"

Here's the truth: clarity creates freedom.

When you have a clear ME Factor, you build a loyal readership who trusts you. That trust gives you the freedom to evolve, experiment, and expand—because your readers aren't just buying a genre from you. They're buying your sensibility, your voice, your perspective.

Authors with vague positioning struggle to build any readership at all—because no one knows what to expect from them. Authors with clear positioning build loyal fans who will follow them across genres because they trust the visionary, the voice behind the work.

HOW: Discovering Your ME Factor

Discovering your ME Factor isn't about inventing something new. It's about uncovering what's already there—the patterns, themes, and elements that make your work recognizable.

Step 1: Define Your Goal

What do you want your writing career to accomplish?

This isn't about what you "should" want. It's an honest self-assessment. Different goals require different strategies, so clarity here shapes everything else.

Possible goals:

- Build a full-time income from writing
- Create a body of work that explores specific themes
- Establish authority and thought leadership in your field
- Build a passionate reader community
- Achieve critical recognition or literary awards
- Maintain creative freedom while earning supplemental income

Your goal isn't right or wrong—it's yours. Document this. Be specific.

Step 2: Identify Your Audience

Who are you writing for? Not in theory—in reality.

Don't say "everyone who likes thrillers" or "all leaders." That's not an audience. That's a market segment containing millions of people with wildly different tastes.

Fiction example: "Professional women 35-50 who read to decompress and want smart, fast-paced psychological suspense with strong female leads."

Nonfiction example: "First-time VPs (35-45) navigating the jump from manager to executive, looking for honest guidance on corporate politics and influence—not platitudes."

The more specific you are, the clearer your positioning becomes.

Ask yourself:

- What age range and life stage are my ideal readers in?
- What are they seeking emotionally/professionally when they pick up a book like mine?

- What do they love that I can deliver? What do they hate that I can avoid?

Step 3: Discover What Makes YOU Distinct

This is the hardest part because it requires seeing yourself clearly—something writers notoriously struggle with. The same sensitivity that makes you a good writer—the ability to see nuance, question everything, consider multiple perspectives —can make it harder to see your own distinct value.

You're looking for the elements that make your work unmistakably yours:

Your Voice: How you tell stories or present ideas. Are you lyrical or spare? Darkly funny or deadly serious? Data-driven or narrative-focused?

Your Themes: What you consistently explore. Justice, belonging, power, resilience, identity, morality, systemic change, ethical leadership. What are your recurring preoccupations?

Your Expertise: What insider knowledge or lived experience do you bring?

- Fiction: A prosecutor writing legal thrillers. A therapist writing psychological suspense.
- Nonfiction: A Chief Human Resources Officer writing about organizational culture. A neuroscientist writing about productivity.

Your Emotional Signature: The feeling readers get from your work. Do they finish feeling hopeful? Unsettled? Cathartic? Empowered? This is your emotional brand.

To identify your YOU elements, ask:

1. What do readers consistently praise about my work?
2. What themes do I return to again and again?
3. What lived experience or expertise do I bring that most authors don't?
4. If someone read my book without seeing my name, what would make them think it's mine?

Step 4: Apply the Formula

Now combine the three elements:

Goal + Audience + YOU = Your ME Factor

Fiction Example:

- Goal: Build viable income writing books I'm passionate about
- Audience: Readers 30-55 who love smart, atmospheric thrillers with morally complex characters
- YOU: Former FBI analyst; fascinated by institutional corruption; tight, procedural plots with insider authenticity

ME Factor: "I write intelligence-driven thrillers for readers who want insider authenticity and morally gray protagonists navigating institutional corruption."

Nonfiction Example:

- Goal: Establish thought leadership and open doors for speaking and consulting
- Audience: Mid-career managers (30-45) navigating

toxic work cultures
- YOU: Former VP of HR; 15 years in corporate culture transformation; frameworks-driven; no-BS tone

ME Factor: "I write for mid-career managers stuck in toxic work cultures, offering battle-tested frameworks for reclaiming agency—from someone who's been in the trenches, not just the boardroom."

See how each ME Factor is specific, clear, and distinct? You know exactly who the author is, who they serve, and what makes them different.

Step 5: Test and Refine

Your first ME Factor draft won't be perfect. That's okay. You're looking for clarity, not poetry.

Test it by asking:

- Can I say this in one breath without rambling?
- Does it sound like me, or does it sound like marketing copy?
- Would this help a reader decide if my book is for them?
- Does it differentiate me from other authors in my space?

Refine until it feels true, clear, and specific. You'll know you've landed on it when someone says, "Oh, I need to read your books" or "That's not for me, but I know who would love it." Both responses mean your positioning is working.

CALIBRATION: Testing if Your ME Factor is Truly Differentiated

How do you know if your ME Factor is distinct—or just a slightly reworded version of what everyone else is saying?

Warning Signs:

✖ **The Substitution Test fails**: Take your ME Factor statement and remove your name. Could it describe five other authors? If yes, it's not differentiated enough. *Return to Step 3 and dig deeper—what specific combination of elements is uniquely yours?*

✖ **The Stranger Test fails**: You deliver your ME Factor at an event. They respond with "Oh... cool" and look confused. This means your positioning is vague. *Don't worry—this just means you need to get more specific. Try adding concrete details about your emotional signature or reader experience.*

✖ **You can't name comp titles or explain how you're different**: If you can't say "I'm like X author but with Y difference," you don't yet understand your positioning. *Chapter 4 will teach you competitive benchmarking—you'll learn how to identify your comp titles and articulate your distinctions clearly.*

✖ **Your content strategy isn't obvious**: Based on your ME Factor, you should be able to immediately identify 3-5 content pillars for social media. If you can't, your ME Factor isn't clear enough. *Keep reading—Chapter 8 walks you through building content pillars directly from your ME Factor.*

Good Signs:

✔ **You can articulate your positioning in one sentence** that's specific, grounded in market understanding, and clearly differentiates you.

✓ **Content creation feels easier** because you have clear focus about what to talk about and why.

✓ **You know you're attracting the right readers** because they "get" what you do immediately.

✓ **People can describe your work to others accurately** without seeing your marketing materials.

The Three-Month Test

After using your ME Factor for three months:

Warning signs:

- You're still attracting random, mismatched readers
- Content creation still feels scattered
- People seem confused when you describe your work
- You feel like you're performing a persona

Good signs:

- You're attracting readers who match your target persona
- Content flows naturally from your positioning
- People describe your work accurately to others
- You feel more confident introducing yourself as an author

If the warning signs persist, revisit your ME Factor. Something isn't aligned—usually it's trying to be what you think you "should" be rather than owning what you are. And that's okay

—this is iterative work.

WORKROOM: Discovering Your ME Factor

LEVEL 1: ESSENTIAL (Start here) – 30 minutes

Your Goal: What do I want my writing career to accomplish in the next 3-5 years?

Your Audience: Who am I writing for? (Be specific: age, life stage, what they're seeking, what they love/avoid)

What Makes YOU Distinct:

- Themes I consistently explore:
- Expertise or lived experience I bring:
- My emotional signature (how readers feel after finishing):

Draft Your ME Factor:

Fiction: "I write [type of book] for [specific audience] who want [specific emotional experience], bringing [what makes you unique]."

Nonfiction: "I help/write for [specific audience] [facing what challenge] through [your approach], bringing [your unique expertise/perspective]."

First draft:

LEVEL 2: IF YOU WANT TO GO DEEPER (Optional)

Test Your ME Factor:

Substitution Test: Could this describe other authors? If yes, make it more specific.

Comp Title Test: Name 3-5 authors/books similar to yours and explain how you're different.

Content Pillar Test: Based on my ME Factor, what are 3-5 topics I should consistently talk about on social media?

Refined ME Factor:

Your ME Factor isn't permanent. It will evolve as you publish more books and grow as a writer. But you need a starting point —a clear positioning statement that guides your decisions today.

Once you have your ME Factor, everything else becomes easier. Your market intelligence efforts become focused. Your brand pillars emerge naturally. Your platform strategy becomes obvious.

This is your foundation. Build it well. And remember: clarity creates freedom. When you know who you are and who you serve, you can turn 'being everything to everyone' into being unmistakably you.

CHAPTER 3

THE EMOTIONAL PROMISE: WHAT READERS COME BACK FOR

Most authors break promises they never knew they made.

Name it, and suddenly everything—your brand, your platform, your next book—snaps into focus.

You might think your book is about a detective solving a murder, or a CEO navigating a merger, or a woman rebuilding her life after loss. But underneath the plot, beneath the information and advice, there's something deeper happening: you're making an emotional promise.

Readers don't buy books for what happens on the page. They buy books for how those pages will make them *feel*.

A thriller reader isn't just buying a mystery to solve—they're buying the rush of tension and the satisfaction of justice. A romance reader isn't just buying a love story—they're buying hope, escape, and the guarantee of a happy ending. A business book reader isn't just buying frameworks—they're buying confidence, clarity, and the feeling that change is possible.

Your emotional promise is the feeling readers can count on receiving from your work. It's what makes them come back book after book, even when the plots change or the topics shift. It's the through-line that connects everything you write—the feeling that makes your readers say, "This is why I read this author."

And here's what most authors miss: if you don't understand your emotional promise, you can't deliver it consistently. You'll write books that confuse your audience, build a platform that feels disconnected from your work, and wonder why readers who loved your first book didn't connect with your second.

This chapter helps you identify and articulate your emotional promise so you can deliver it with intention, build reader loyalty that lasts, and create a career where every book strengthens your position instead of starting over.

WHAT: Understanding the Emotional Promise

Your emotional promise is what allows readers to stop evaluating and start surrendering to your work.

The emotional promise isn't primarily a marketing tool—it's a reading experience that allows readers to give themselves over to your work completely. When you break that promise, readers approach your next book with suspicion - one foot out the door, waiting to see if you'll deliver or disappoint. But when you deliver it consistently? That's when casual readers become devoted fans.

Your emotional promise is the consistent emotional experience readers can expect from your work. It's not the plot, the genre, or even the themes—it's the *feeling* readers take away after closing your book.

Think of it this way: when someone finishes one of your books, what feeling do you want them to remember days or weeks later?

Fiction examples:

- **Hopeful despite darkness**: Your stories explore difficult topics—trauma, injustice, loss—but readers always close the book feeling like resilience is possible.
- **Intellectually satisfied**: Your plots are intricate puzzles. Readers finish feeling smart for following the threads, excited by what they've learned, impressed by the construction.
- **Thrillingly unsettled**: You write endings that refuse easy resolution. Readers finish unsettled in the best way —thinking, questioning, slightly unnerved but wholly engaged.

Nonfiction examples:

- **Empowered and capable**: Your frameworks make complex challenges feel manageable. Readers finish believing they can do this.
- **Validated and understood**: You name experiences others dismiss. Readers finish feeling seen, less alone.

- **Challenged and expanded**: You push readers to question assumptions. They finish uncomfortable in a productive way—their worldview has shifted.

Notice that none of these are about genre or topic. A psychological thriller and a memoir about grief could both deliver "hopeful despite darkness." A business book about negotiation and a self-help book about boundaries could both deliver "empowered and capable."

Your emotional promise transcends genre—it's your signature feeling.

WHY: Emotional Consistency in an Unpredictable Market

The publishing market is brutal in its unpredictability. Algorithm changes tank visibility overnight. Trends shift without warning. You can't control any of it.

But here's what you *can* control: the emotional experience you create through your books.

In a market where readers are overwhelmed by choice and algorithms dictate discovery, your emotional promise becomes your competitive advantage. It's the reason readers seek you out specifically, recommend you passionately, and return reliably.

The Data: Readers who have bought and read 2+ books by an author are 61% more likely to purchase their next release, compared to readers discovering the author for the first time. That consistent emotional delivery builds successful careers.

The Reader Psychology Behind Emotional Promises

Readers don't just buy books—they buy emotional experiences they need at specific moments in their lives.

Someone going through a difficult time might seek books that promise "hopeful despite darkness"—they need to believe survival is possible. Someone burnt out at work might seek "validated and understood"—they need to feel less alone. Someone facing a major life transition might seek 'reassured'—they need to know they're not making a mistake.

When your emotional promise is clear, readers can self-select. They know whether your books will meet their emotional needs right now. This is why some readers devour your entire backlist in a week, while others respect your work but say "not for me"—and both responses indicate strong positioning.

When your emotional promise is vague or inconsistent, readers gamble. They might try one book and love it, then try another and feel betrayed because it delivered a completely different emotional experience. They don't come back—not because the second book was bad, but because they can't trust what they'll get from you. This is common, and fixable. When you define your emotional promise clearly (which you'll do in this chapter), your readers will know exactly what to expect.

For Business Executives Writing Nonfiction

You understand this from your corporate experience. A strong brand delivers a consistent promise—Volvo promises safety, Apple promises innovation. Customers return because they trust that promise will be kept.

Your author brand works the same way. If your first book promised "validated and understood," your second book needs to deliver that same emotional core—even if the topics differ. The executives who successfully build thought leadership platforms aren't always writing about the same topic—they're delivering the same emotional experience consistently.

For Fiction Writers Across Genres

Your emotional promise is what allows you to grow your career without being trapped by genre conventions.

If your emotional promise is "intellectually satisfied," you can write literary fiction, historical mystery, or speculative fiction —as long as each delivers that intricate, puzzle-like satisfaction. Your readers follow you because they trust the feeling, not the genre label.

If your emotional promise is "warm and restored," you can write romance, women's fiction, or even cozy mystery—as long as readers finish feeling safe and connected. The genre is just the vehicle for delivering the emotion you're known for.

The Long Game

In a market where millions of books compete annually, differentiation isn't optional. But most authors differentiate on surface elements—genre, setting, character types—that are easily replicated.

Your emotional promise is deeper – and it's the differentiation that's nearly impossible to copy. It comes from who you are, what you've lived, what you care about, and how you see the world. Another author can write in your genre, use similar tropes, even copy your cover aesthetic. But they can't replicate your emotional signature.

This is your moat. Build it intentionally.

HOW: Discovering Your Emotional Promise

Most authors don't consciously choose their emotional promise —it emerges from their writing instinctively. Your job isn't to invent an emotional promise; it's to *recognize* the one already woven through your work.

Step 1: Mine Your Existing Work

If you've already published books, your emotional promise is in the patterns. Look across your body of work and ask:

What do readers consistently say about how my books make them feel?

Don't look at what they say about plot or writing quality. Look specifically for emotional reactions. Pull actual quotes from reviews, emails, and messages. The language readers use reveals your emotional promise.

What emotional notes do I consistently hit across different books?

Even if your plots vary wildly, certain emotional beats likely recur. These patterns point to your core emotional offering.

If you haven't published yet, analyze your current manuscript or your reading preferences:

What books do you return to when you need a specific feeling?

The books you love reveal the emotional experiences you value—and likely the ones you create.

When you imagine a reader finishing your book, what do you want them to feel?

Your answer—your gut, instinctive answer—is probably your emotional promise.

Step 2: Identify Your Emotional Range

Your emotional promise isn't one note. It's a range with a consistent center.

Imagine a color palette. Your emotional promise might be "hopeful despite darkness"—which means your range includes grief, struggle, resilience, and hope. You move through that range, but you always land on the hopeful end.

Map your emotional range by asking:

1. **What's the darkest emotion I explore in my work?** (Grief? Fear? Despair? Cynicism?)
2. **What's the lightest emotion I reach?** (Hope? Joy? Triumph? Peace?)
3. **Where do I consistently land at the end?** (This is your emotional promise—the feeling readers close the book with.)

Fiction example:

- Darkest: Betrayal and moral failure
- Lightest: Justice (earned, not easy)
- Emotional promise: "Hopeful despite moral complexity"

Nonfiction example:

- Darkest: Overwhelm and systemic barriers
- Lightest: Strategic clarity and agency
- Emotional promise: "Empowered despite constraints"

Step 3: Name Your Emotional Promise

Using the patterns you've identified, craft a short phrase that captures your emotional promise. This is for your own clarity —you won't necessarily use this language in marketing, but it guides every decision you make and is worthy of a place on your whiteboard.

Fiction formula: "My books make readers feel [primary emotion] through [what you explore]."

Examples:

- "My books make readers feel intellectually satisfied through intricate plotting and layered reveals."
- "My books make readers feel hopeful despite darkness through characters who find meaning in struggle."

Nonfiction formula: "My books make readers feel [primary emotion] by [how you deliver value]."

Examples:

- "My books make readers feel empowered and capable by breaking complex challenges into clear, actionable frameworks."
- "My books make readers feel validated and understood by naming experiences others overlook or dismiss."

Step 4: Test Against Your ME Factor

Your emotional promise should align with your ME Factor (from Chapter 2). They reinforce each other.

If your ME Factor is: "I write corporate espionage thrillers for readers who want insider authenticity and morally gray protagonists"

Your emotional promise might be: "Intellectually satisfied through complex moral navigation"

If your ME Factor is: "I help first-time VPs navigate executive politics through systems thinking"

Your emotional promise might be: "Strategically confident despite organizational chaos"

Alignment check: Can you see how your ME Factor (who you are and who you serve) naturally produces your emotional promise (how readers feel)? If not, one of them needs adjustment.

Step 5: Validate with Readers

Once you've identified your emotional promise, test it against reader feedback—not by asking them directly (most readers can't articulate it), but by checking if your language matches their experience.

Go back to reviews, emails, or beta reader feedback. Do readers describe feelings that align with your identified emotional promise?

If you said your emotional promise is "intellectually satisfied" but reviews consistently mention "emotional catharsis," your self-assessment is off. Trust what readers report feeling— they're telling you your actual emotional promise.

CALIBRATION: Signs Your Emotional Promise is Clear and Consistent

How do you know if you're delivering your emotional promise effectively—or if you're confusing readers with mixed signals?

Warning Signs:

✖ **Readers describe different emotional experiences across your backlist**

This means you're not delivering a consistent emotional promise. Readers don't know what to expect from you, which kills series momentum.

✖ **Your platform content feels disconnected from your books**

Your books explore dark themes and moral ambiguity, but your social media is sunshine and inspiration. Misalignment makes readers question whether they know you.

✖ **You can't describe your emotional promise without**

using plot details

"My books are about a detective solving crimes" is plot. "My books make readers feel justice is possible even in corrupt systems" is emotional promise.

✘ Readers who loved your first book don't automatically buy your second

This is the clearest signal that your emotional promise isn't consistent.

Good Signs:

✔ Readers use similar emotional language across reviews of different books

"Another book that left me feeling hopeful!" means you're delivering your emotional promise consistently.

✔ Your platform content naturally evokes the same emotional tone as your books

If your books deliver "intellectually satisfied," your posts explore craft and complexity. There's coherence—and it feels effortless.

✔ You can describe your emotional promise in one sentence

If you can say it clearly, you understand it—and can deliver it intentionally.

✔ New readers who discover you through one book often

binge your backlist

When readers connect with your emotional promise in one book, they trust it enough to invest in your entire catalog.

✔ **Your writing process feels aligned with your marketing**

You're not writing one kind of book and then struggling to market it. Everything flows from the same source.

The Three-Month Check-In

After implementing clarity around your emotional promise for three months, ask:

1. Do I feel more confident describing my work?
2. Does content creation feel easier?
3. Are readers describing my work more consistently?
4. Am I attracting readers who "get" me?

If you answered "no" to most of these, that's okay – this is iterative work. Revisit Step 1: you might be projecting what you *think* your emotional promise should be rather than recognizing what it is. Go back to reader feedback. Trust what they report feeling.

WORKROOM: Defining Your Emotional Promise

LEVEL 1: ESSENTIAL (Start here) – 30 minutes

Part 1: Mining Your Emotional Patterns

If you've published: Pull 10-15 reader reviews. Highlight every phrase where readers describe how your book made them *feel*.

What emotions do readers consistently report?

If you haven't yet published: Think about the last 5-10 books you loved. For each, write down the primary emotion you felt after finishing.

What patterns do you see in your own reading?

Part 2: Mapping Your Emotional Range

What's the darkest emotion I explore in my work?

What's the lightest/most hopeful emotion I reach?

Where do I consistently land at the end?

Part 3: Draft Your Emotional Promise Statement

For fiction: "My books make readers feel [primary emotion] through [what you explore]."

For nonfiction: "My books make readers feel [primary emotion] by [how you deliver value]."

First draft:

LEVEL 2: IF YOU WANT TO GO DEEPER (Optional)

Alignment Check:

Does this emotional promise align with my ME Factor from Chapter 2?

Reader Validation:

Pull 5-10 pieces of reader feedback. Do readers report feeling what you identified?

What readers report feeling:

Revised emotional promise (if needed):

Platform Alignment Planning:

Based on my emotional promise, what tone should my platform content have?

Three content themes that align with my emotional promise: 1. 2. 3.

Your emotional promise is the invisible thread connecting everything you write. Once you can name it, you can deliver it intentionally—which means every book strengthens your brand, every reader becomes more loyal, and your career builds momentum instead of resetting with each release.

This isn't about manipulating reader emotions. It's about honoring what you naturally create and ensuring readers can find the emotional impact they need from you.

You've defined your ME Factor (who you are and who you serve). You've identified your emotional promise (how readers feel). Now you have the foundation for everything that follows: market intelligence that's focused, brand strategy that's coherent, and platform decisions that feel authentic.

In Chapter 4, we'll take this internal clarity and turn it outward —to understand where you fit in the competitive landscape and how to position yourself strategically. Because knowing who you are is essential, but knowing where you stand in the market is what turns identity into visibility.

You're building the foundation for a well-supported writing career. One clear decision at a time.

PART II

THE INTELLIGENCE: FINDING YOUR PLACE IN THE MARKET

Once you know who you are, you'll use key data to map exactly where you fit in the crowded landscape.

If you're writing or marketing your first book: This section prevents the #1 mistake new authors make—positioning too broadly. You'll identify exactly where you fit before investing months of effort reaching the wrong segment of readers.

If you've published but struggle to gain traction: This section diagnoses the problem. You'll discover whether your issue is positioning (wrong audience), messaging (unclear differentiation), or market gap (oversaturated space)—and create a clear path forward.

If you're returning after a break: Reader behavior may have shifted dramatically since you last published. This section shows you what's changed in your genre's landscape, where new opportunities exist, and how to position yourself strategically in today's market.

CHAPTER 4

MARKET INTELLIGENCE: KNOW WHERE YOU FIT

What if market intelligence wasn't tedious analysis—but creative strategy that simplified positioning?

Most authors want to understand their market—they're just not sure how. So they rely on what's visible: scrolling through BookTok, watching what goes viral on Instagram, asking other authors what worked for them. You're already gathering market intelligence. Now let's organize it into a decision-making tool.

Your creative instinct is essential. It's what makes your work yours. But instinct alone can't tell you which Amazon categories your readers browse, what language they use when recommending books they love, or where the underserved gaps are in your market.

This chapter teaches you how to gather market intelligence that's actionable—not overwhelming. You'll learn where you fit competitively, what makes you different from similar authors, what readers in your space are seeking, and where opportunities exist that your work can fill.

The good news? This is simpler than it sounds. No expensive tools. No research degree. Just focused observation using free resources you already use.

WHAT: Market Intelligence for Authors

It sounds intimidating. It's not.

Using simple methods, you'll be observing patterns, listening to readers, and understanding your competitive landscape.

Market intelligence means understanding:

Your competitive set: Who are you really competing with? Not every author in your genre—your specific subset based on tone, themes, and emotional promise.

Example: If you write cozy mysteries, your competitive set isn't *all* cozy mystery authors. It's specifically cozy mysteries with bookstore settings and older protagonists. That's maybe 200 authors—manageable. If you're a business executive writing about organizational change, your competitive set isn't *all* business books—it's books about change management for mid-size companies or specific industries. That narrows the field dramatically.

What makes YOU different: Once you know your targeted competitive set, you need to understand your specific advantage. What do you offer that others don't? This is competitive benchmarking—identifying your uniqueness.

Reader expectations: What are readers in your space looking for? What language do they use? Where do they hang out?

Market gaps: Where is demand not being met? What are readers asking for that they can't find from other authors or books?

Trends vs. fads: What's sustainable versus what's temporary?

Market intelligence is not copying bestsellers, writing to trends instead of your authentic voice, or letting data override your creative vision. It's understanding your context so you can position strategically, speaking the language your readers use, and finding the readers who will love what you write.

And here's the reassuring part: you probably already do much of this instinctively. When you read books in your genre and think "readers would love more of this," that's market intelligence. This chapter just gives you a simple framework for using it intentionally and as part of a sophisticated system.

Five Simple Components

1. Competition: What are your comp titles? Books that serve the same reader need with a similar emotional promise.

2. Your Competitive Edge: What makes YOU different from those comp titles? This is where benchmarking comes in.

3. Your Readers: What do your ideal readers want? What

language do they use?

4. What's Trending: What's emerging and powerful versus what's fading?

5. Where Are the Gaps: Where is demand exceeding supply?

You don't need to do all of this at once. Competition is the easiest entry point, then you'll add more as you go. Each component gives you more clarity for better understanding of the big picture.

Key Point: You don't need to become a market analyst to use and leverage market intelligence tactics. You're just using them to position your work where your readers can find it.

WHY: The Power of Knowing vs. The Cost of Guessing

Most authors operate on assumptions:

- "My book is for readers who love [bestselling author]"
- "My readers are probably on Instagram"
- "If I write a great book, readers will find it"

Some of these might be true. But when they're wrong, you waste time, money, and energy on strategies that don't work.

The Data: Authors using strategic market intelligence are 45% more likely to outperform competitors in revenue and engagement.

The gap between talented authors who either struggle or thrive isn't the quality of their work—it's whether they understand why, how, and where that work fits and who's looking for it.

What Happens Without Market Intelligence

Fiction example: You write a dark, literary thriller with an ambiguous ending. You position it as "for fans of Gillian Flynn" because she writes thrillers. But Flynn's readers expect twisty plots with clear resolutions. Your book is closer to Tana French—atmospheric, literary, morally complex. By positioning incorrectly, you attract the wrong readers (who leave disappointed reviews) and never reach the right readers who would love your work.

An hour reading reviews would have shown you this mismatch before your book launch.

Nonfiction example: A productivity expert positions her work "for ambitious professionals who want to achieve more." Yet her methodology is really designed for people with ADHD who often adapt themselves to work environments not designed with their needs in mind. By positioning too broadly, she misses the readers who would benefit most and instead attracts others who experience the guidance as overly detailed, even though that level of specificity is essential for the audience it was created to serve.

These aren't failures of talent or expertise. They're positioning mismatches that more attentive market insight can prevent.

What Market Intelligence Makes Possible

When you understand your market, you start to feel more confident about every decision you make about your writing career.

Fiction example: A debut thriller author spends a few hours analyzing her comp titles. She notices successful books in her subgenre all use single-word titles and dark, minimalist covers. She had planned a three-word title with a bright cover. By modifying her cover to match category signals (while keeping her unique voice), the click-through rate on her Amazon book page increases by 65%. But more importantly, she identifies what makes her different: her background as a forensic psychologist gives her insider authenticity that most thriller authors don't have. That detail – her ME Factor - becomes her competitive edge.

Nonfiction example: A leadership consultant analyzes his comp titles and notices most leadership books are intended for an audience of Fortune 500 executives. But his expertise is leading mid-size nonprofit organizations—completely different constraints and culture. By positioning specifically for nonprofit leaders navigating change with limited budgets and consensus-driven cultures, he claims an underserved niche and becomes the go-to expert in that space.

These authors carefully observed, understood patterns, identified their unique advantage, and positioned their authentic work where the right readers were already looking.

For Business Executives

You already know how to do this. You've done SWOT analyses, competitive positioning, customer discovery interviews. Your book is a product. Your readers are your customers. Same strategic thinking, new context. The frameworks you know translate directly—you're just applying them to the world of publishing instead of global business operations.

For Fiction Writers

Market intelligence isn't about compromising your vision. It's about understanding where your authentic work fits so the right readers can find it. You're already observing patterns when you read—this chapter just gives you a framework to organize those observations strategically.

HOW: Gathering Market Intelligence

Market intelligence breaks down into manageable steps. Start where it feels easiest, build from there.

Step 1: Find Your Comp Titles (30 minutes)

Comp titles are books similar to yours in tone, themes, and emotional promise—not just genre.

How to find them:

1. Start with 2-3 books that feel similar to yours
2. Use Amazon's "Customers also bought" feature—see what else readers are buying
3. Check Goodreads lists—see what readers are grouping together
4. Narrow to 5-6 strong comps (published in the last 3-5 years, performing well but not blockbusters)

Fiction example: A thriller author starts with Tana French, checks her "also boughts," and discovers readers also buy Megan Miranda and Laura McHugh. She narrows to 6 comp titles that all deliver "slow-burn psychological tension with literary prose."

Nonfiction example: A business author checks "also boughts" for books about emotional intelligence in leadership and discovers a cluster of readers who want vulnerability paired with practical business application—not just inspirational storytelling.

This is a doable, bite-sized analysis that's packed with potential value. Instead of analyzing the entire market, you're finding 5-6 books that occupy a similar space to yours.

Step 2: Notice Patterns (30 minutes)

Look at your comp titles and notice:

Covers: What colors? What imagery? What typography?

Titles: Single words? Phrases? What's the pattern?

Book descriptions: How are they structured? What language do they use?

Categories: What Amazon categories are they in?

Pricing: What do they cost? Compare not only the price but also the number of pages to get the full picture.

Reviews: Read 10-15 reviews total. What do readers consistently praise? What do they complain about?

Fiction example: A romance author notices her comp titles all use illustrated covers with warm colors, 2-3 word titles, pricing the Kindle versions at $2.99 - $4.99, and readers consistently praise "banter" and "slow burn."

Nonfiction example: A business book author notices his comp titles all use two-word titles, minimal covers with bold typography, and readers praise "actionable frameworks" and "no corporate BS."

This analysis helps you understand the signals that tell readers "this book is for you."

Step 3: Identify Your Competitive Edge (Benchmarking - 30 minutes)

Now that you know your competitive set, ask: **What makes ME different?**

This is competitive benchmarking—identifying what you offer that your competitors don't.

Look for:

Unique expertise or experience: What do you bring that most authors in your space don't?

- Fiction: An EMT writing medical thrillers. A high school teacher writing YA contemporary about classroom dynamics. A chef writing culinary cozy mysteries.
- Nonfiction: A former customer service manager writing about leadership. A social worker writing about burnout prevention. An IT Manager writing about network optimization.

Different angle on familiar topics: Same general category, but a fresh perspective.

- Fiction: Thrillers set in academia vs. domestic settings. Romance featuring older protagonists vs. twenty-somethings.
- Nonfiction: Leadership for first-generation professionals vs. general leadership. Burnout-free productivity vs. efficiency-oriented productivity about working smarter.

Your authentic background or perspective: What lived experience informs your work?

- Fiction: Your cultural heritage, regional setting, or life experience that brings fresh authenticity to your genre
- Nonfiction: Your professional background, personal challenges you've navigated, or real-world experience that makes your guidance credible

Different emotional promise: You deliver a feeling your comp titles don't (see Chapter 3).

Example - Fiction: A mystery author's comp titles all feature amateur sleuths who stumble into investigations. Her protagonist is a former detective who left the force after a scandal—she brings procedural expertise and explores institutional corruption. That's her edge: insider authenticity and moral complexity that cozy mystery readers aren't getting elsewhere.

Example - Nonfiction: A productivity author's comp titles all assume readers have schedule control. His expertise is productivity for shift workers, healthcare professionals, and others with inflexible schedules. That's his edge: practical strategies for people the other books ignore.

The key question: "Readers who love [my comp titles] but wish they had more [X] will love my work because I offer [X]."

This is your positioning statement. This is how you differentiate.

Step 4: Listen to Readers (30 minutes)

Readers tell you exactly what they want if you know where to listen.

Reviews: Read reviews of your comp titles on Amazon and Goodreads. Pull exact quotes about what readers loved and wished for, but pay closer attention to what they didn't get. This is valuable intel.

Communities: Spend a week observing 1-2 reader communities (Goodreads groups, Facebook groups, subreddits). What are they discussing? What are they seeking?

Fiction example: A fantasy author reads 30 reviews and notices readers praise "morally gray characters" and "world-building without info-dumps" while complaining about "too many POVs." From that, she knows what to deliver, what to avoid, and the exact words to use in her book description.

Nonfiction example: An author writing about career transitions observes posts in professional communities and notices repeated frustration with advice that assumes freedom to relocate, unlimited networking time, or no caregiving responsibilities. She positions her book for people navigating career transitions with real constraints.

You're not interrupting anyone by conducting personal surveys

—you're just listening online to what readers openly share.

Beyond understanding your readers, these phrases become your keywords. **SEO (Search Engine Optimization)** means using these keywords strategically on your website and in book descriptions so search engines connect you to people searching for books like yours. **Keywords** are the phrases readers type into Google: "psychological thriller unreliable narrator" or "productivity books for executives." Save the phrases you're capturing - you'll use them in Chapter 9 when building your website.

Step 5: Find the Gaps (20 minutes)

Look for what readers are asking for but not finding:

- What do reviews say readers "wish" existed?
- What recommendations do readers struggle to find in communities?

Fiction example: An author notices repeated requests in fantasy communities for "fantasy without chosen-one narratives—just competent people navigating challenges." Her manuscript featuring a seasoned warrior navigating political intrigue fills this gap.

Nonfiction example: A financial advisor notices most money books target either young professionals or high-net-worth individuals. There's a gap for people in their 40s-50s managing multi-generational financial complexity. That's her niche: the "sandwich generation" financial guide.

You're not changing your voice to fill a gap—you're recognizing where your authentic work meets genuine, underserved demand and using that knowledge as part of your strategy.

CALIBRATION: Is Your Market Intelligence Working?

Warning Signs:

✗ You feel paralyzed by too much information

Solution: Start smaller. Pick 3-4 comp titles, not 10. Focus on one component at a time.

✗ You're doubting your creative vision

Solution: Market intelligence should clarify where YOUR work fits—not tell you to write someone else's book. Refocus your research on finding books similar to yours, while appreciating your unique voice and its integral place in the literary market.

✗ You're copying instead of adapting

Solution: Ask: "Does this serve MY readers and MY positioning?" If not, don't force it.

✗ You can't articulate your competitive edge

Solution: Go back to Step 3. What do you offer that your comp titles don't? What makes you different, not just similar?

Good Signs:

✔ You can clearly articulate your positioning in one sentence

"I write atmospheric psychological thrillers set in academia for readers who love Tana French—but want insider authenticity from a former professor."

✔ **You can explain your competitive advantage**

"Most leadership books assume their readers are Fortune 500 executives. I write for nonprofit leaders navigating change with limited budgets and consensus-driven cultures."

✔ **Your messaging uses real-world language that readers use**

You're using words pulled directly from reviews and community discussions.

✔ **You're attracting the right readers**

The people engaging with your content match your target audience.

✔ **You feel more confident, not more anxious**

The intelligence gathering reduced uncertainty rather than creating more.

WORKROOM: Your Market Intelligence Starter Kit

LEVEL 1: ESSENTIAL (Start here) – 30 minutes

Find 3-5 Comp Titles:

Go to Amazon. Find one book similar to yours. Scroll down the page to find the "Customers also bought" section. Document 3-5 titles.

Your comp titles:

1.

2.

3.

4.

5.

Notice ONE Pattern:

Look at covers: What's the dominant visual pattern?

- Color palette:
- Typography:

Look at titles: What's the structure?

Pick ONE Amazon category your comps share:

Identify Your Competitive Edge:

What do I offer that my comp titles don't?

- Unique expertise:
- Different angle:
- Authentic background perspective:
- Emotional promise

My positioning: "Readers who love [comp titles] but wish they had [X] will love my work because I offer [X]."

LEVEL 2: IF YOU WANT TO GO DEEPER (Optional)

Read Reviews:

Pick 2-3 comp titles. Read 10 reviews each. Pull 5 quotes about what readers loved.

Reader language I should use:

1.

2.

3.

4.

5.

Find Your Readers:

Search for ONE community where your comp titles are discussed. Spend 15 minutes observing.

Where do my readers hang out?

What are they looking for?

LEVEL 3: DEEP DIVE (Come back over weeks/months)

Full Analysis:

For each comp, track:

- Cover design
- Title structure
- Amazon categories
- Price point (with page numbers for an accurate comparison)
- Top reader praise
- Where author is visible

Keyword Tracking (Ongoing): As you read reviews and observe communities, save reader phrases in a simple document. Track 15-20 phrases readers use to describe books like yours. You'll use these for your website (Chapter 9) and Amazon (Chapter 14).

Gap Analysis:

What's oversaturated in my category?

What are readers asking for that they're not finding?

What niche can I own?

Market intelligence transforms guessing into strategy. It's accessible—no expensive tools required. Just focused observation and willingness to learn from what readers are already telling you.

You've defined who you are (ME Factor), what you promise emotionally (Emotional Promise), and now you understand where you fit competitively (Market Intelligence & Competitive Edge). Each layer of clarity makes the next decisions easier.

In Chapter 5, we'll focus on understanding your readers at a deeper level—building reader personas that will help you make strategic decisions about content, platform, and outreach.

You're building a foundation that's bringing you closer to your goals, closer to *yourself*, and every chapter makes the next one clearer.

CHAPTER 5

AUDIENCE INSIGHTS & READER PERSONAS

Understanding your readers isn't about demographics and data—it's about connection.

What if you could write your book description, choose your platforms, and create your content with total confidence because you knew who you were talking to? Not "women 25-40 who love fantasy novels"—but real people with specific needs, preferences, and reading habits you understand deeply.

That's what reader personas make possible. This chapter shows you how to build 2-3 reader personas and use them to create customized, targeted content those readers will love, posted on the platforms where they discover books. When you do this well, you become familiar, recognizable, and memorable to exactly the readers who will love your work. They get curious. They look you up. They buy your books.

Reader personas aren't abstract marketing exercises—they're strategic tools that connect everything: who you're writing for, what content resonates with them, where to reach them, and how to turn curiosity into book sales and long-term loyalty.

And here's the best part: you don't need focus groups or market research firms. You just need to pay attention to what readers are already telling you.

WHAT: Reader Personas That Work

A reader persona is a detailed profile of your ideal reader based on real patterns you've observed—not assumptions.

You'll build 2-3 personas: your primary reader (the person most likely to love your work and tell others about it) and 1-2 secondary readers who also connect with what you create.

Each persona includes:

Demographics: Age, life stage, gender, location, occupation—but this is just the starting point.

Psychographics: Values, interests, challenges, emotional needs, reading motivations.

Behavioral patterns: Where they discover books, how they decide what to read, when they read, buying habits, what makes them recommend books to others.

Reading preferences: Pacing, tone, themes they love, tropes they avoid, what makes them finish or abandon books.

Platform habits: What social media they use, what content they engage with, where they spend their online time.

Language they use: The actual words and phrases they use when describing books they love—this becomes your marketing language.

Why Reader Personas Matter

When you understand your readers at this level, everything becomes clearer and more strategic:

Your content strategy writes itself because you know what topics, tone, and format resonate with your personas.

Your platform choices become obvious because you know where your readers spend time.

Your book descriptions convert better because you're speaking directly to what your readers seek, using language they recognize.

You stop spreading yourself thin trying to be everywhere and focus energy where it will reach your readers.

You build familiarity and recognition by consistently showing up where your readers are with content they care about—which leads to curiosity, discovery, and book sales.

Reader personas turn scattered effort into strategic action.

WHY: What Becomes Possible with Reader Understanding

Most authors define their audience too broadly: Readers who like romance. Business professionals. Anyone who enjoys a good mystery.

These definitions don't help you make strategic decisions. Should you be on TikTok or Goodreads? Should your cover be bold or minimalist? Should you create video content or written posts? Generic audience definitions can't answer these questions.

Why does this matter?

The Data: Targeted, data-driven campaigns based on detailed audience profiles have been shown to increase conversions by 25% and boost marketing spend efficiency by 30%. By understanding your readers at this granular level, you're not just guessing what they want—you're making data-driven decisions that significantly impact your bottom line.

Marketing "conversions" are where readers turn passive interest into action. When someone visits your website and signs up for your newsletter, that's a conversion. When a social media follower clicks through to your Amazon page, that's a conversion. When someone purchases your book, that's also a conversion (called a "hard conversion" because it involves a financial transaction). Conversions show you what's working with evidence. If 1,000 people visit your website but only 5 sign up for your email list, that tells you something about your messaging. If 500 Instagram followers never click through to see your books, that's information you can use. You're not guessing anymore—you're measuring. And measurement gives you power to improve.

Specificity isn't limiting—it's clarifying. And clarity converts.

What Happens Without Reader Understanding

Fiction example: A fantasy author assumes her readers are "young adults who like fantasy." She builds a TikTok presence because that's where people say YA readers are. But her actual readers are adults 28-45 who loved fantasy as teens and are returning to the genre seeking complex world-building and mature themes. They discover books through Goodreads, Reddit's r/Fantasy, and fantasy-focused podcasts—not TikTok. She spent six months building presence on the wrong platform.

Thirty minutes of reading reviews would have shown her who her actual readers are and where they spend time.

Nonfiction example: A wellness author assumes her audience is "women interested in self-care." She creates Instagram posts about meditation and journaling. But her actual readers are professional women 35-50 managing chronic stress in high-pressure careers—they need tactical stress management, not aspirational self-care. They're on LinkedIn seeking practical solutions during work breaks, not on Instagram looking at aesthetic flat lays.

Observing where her comp title readers congregate would have revealed the mismatch.

These authors worked hard. They created good content. They just created it for the wrong audience on the wrong platforms.

What Becomes Possible with Reader Understanding

Fiction example: A mystery author builds a detailed persona: Persona Cassandra, 52, nurse practitioner, reads during breaks and before bed to decompress, loves cozy mysteries with community settings and justice without graphic violence, discovers books through library recommendations and cozy mystery Facebook groups, values "comfort read" and "palate cleanser" experiences.

With this clarity, the author's strategy becomes obvious:

- Create content about: community in fiction, cozy mystery recommendations, behind-the-scenes on creating comforting narratives
- Post where Cassandra actually is: Cozy mystery Facebook groups, libraries
- Use Cassandra's language: "comfort read," "cozy community," "justice with heart"
- Result: Cassandra sees content that resonates, recognizes this author understands what she wants, gets curious, checks out the books

Nonfiction example: A leadership consultant defines his persona: Persona James, 41, newly promoted director at nonprofit, managing former peers while learning executive-level responsibilities, feels underprepared for organizational politics, reads business books on weekends and during commute, skeptical of theory without practical application, discovers books through LinkedIn and nonprofit leadership groups.

His strategy flows naturally:

- Create content about: navigating the director transition, managing former peers, practical frameworks for nonprofit contexts

- Post on: LinkedIn (where James seeks professional development)
- Use James's language: "practical," "nonprofit reality," "leading through influence not authority"
- Result: James sees content addressing his exact challenges, recognizes this author understands his context, investigates the book

In both cases, the authors aren't creating random content hoping someone notices. They're strategically creating content that specific personas will love, posting it where those readers gather, building familiarity and recognition that leads to book discovery and sales.

For Business Executives

You already do this in your professional life. You create customer personas, user profiles, stakeholder maps. You know you can't build a product for "everyone"—you need to understand your specific user's pain points, behaviors, and decision-making process.

Your readers are your customers. Same discipline applies. The challenge isn't learning a new skill—it's applying familiar strategic thinking to this new context.

For Fiction Writers

You create detailed character profiles for your novels—their backstories, motivations, fears, desires. You know your protagonist better than you know most real people.

Apply that same depth of understanding to your readers. They're not abstract "audiences"—they're real people with specific needs, preferences, and habits. Understanding them doesn't limit your creativity—it helps you reach the people who will love what you create.

HOW: Building Your Reader Personas

Building reader personas isn't guesswork. It's pattern recognition based on observable data. You'll build 2-3 personas —one primary, 1-2 secondary—based on what you observe about who reads and loves books like yours.

Step 1: Start With What You Know (20 minutes)

If you've published books:

- Who bought and reviewed your books?
- What did they say in reviews about why they connected with your work?
- Who shares your books on social media?
- Who joins your email list?

If you haven't published yet:

- Who loves your comp titles? (Check reviews, Goodreads lists, community discussions)
- What books do YOU love, and who reads those same books?
- Based on your ME Factor and Emotional Promise (Chapters 2-3), who's seeking what you offer?

Record everything you observe:

- Age range and life stage
- Occupation (if relevant to their reading interests)

- What they're seeking emotionally from books like yours
- Where you see them active online
- What language they use when talking about books

This is your starting hypothesis. Now you'll test and refine it.

Step 2: Mine Reviews and Reader Feedback (30 minutes)

Go to Amazon and Goodreads. Read 10-15 reviews of your books (if published) or your comp titles (if not yet published).

Look for patterns in:

Who's reading: Do reviewers mention their age, occupation, life stage? ("As a teacher..." "As someone navigating a career change..." "As a longtime romance reader...")

What they're seeking: What emotional needs does the book meet? ("Perfect escape after stressful days" "Exactly what I needed during transition" "Finally, a book that reflects my experience")

What they value: What specific elements do they praise? (Characters, pacing, authenticity, representation, practical frameworks, satisfying endings)

What they avoid: What do they complain about or warn others about? (Too slow, too graphic, unresolved endings, too theoretical)

What platforms they mention: Do they reference where they found the book or where they'll recommend it? ("My book club will love this" "Sharing in my Goodreads group"

"Recommended by my favorite podcast"

Language they use: Pull direct quotes. These exact words become your content and marketing language.

Example - Fiction: A romance author reads 20 reviews of her comp titles and finds patterns:

- Readers mention "as someone in my 40s" or "finally, characters navigating real life"
- They praise "second-chance romance" and "earned happy endings, not insta-love"
- They value "witty banter" and "slow burn tension"
- They're tired of "love triangles" and "miscommunication as only conflict"
- They mention finding books through: Goodreads romance groups, Smart Bitches Trashy Books blog, romance-focused podcasts
- Language: "swoony but realistic," "made me believe in love again," "comfort read with depth"

This tells her: Primary persona is likely 38-50, values emotional authenticity and humor, wants mature relationship dynamics, discovers books through romance communities and blogs.

Example - Nonfiction: A career strategist reads 20 reviews of comp titles and notices:

- Readers mention "stuck in middle management" or "ready for next level but don't know how"
- They praise "practical steps without corporate BS" and "real examples"
- They're frustrated by advice assuming "unlimited networking time" or "flexible schedule"

- They mention finding books through: LinkedIn recommendations, professional development groups, career-focused podcasts
- Language: "finally, realistic advice," "actionable without being overwhelming," "addresses real barriers"

This tells him: Primary persona is likely 35-48, mid-career professional seeking advancement, constrained by real-world limitations, discovers books through professional networks.

Step 3: Observe Reader Communities (1-2 weeks)

Join 1-2 communities where your readers spend time:

- Goodreads groups for your genre
- Facebook groups for readers of your type of book
- Subreddits (r/Fantasy, r/RomanceBooks, r/books, r/careerguidance, industry-specific subs)
- LinkedIn groups (for nonfiction topics)

Observe without pitching your book:

- What questions do people ask repeatedly?
- What recommendations do they seek?
- What content gets the most engagement?
- What frustrates them about existing options?
- What gets them excited?
- What language and phrases appear repeatedly?

Fiction example: A sci-fi author spends two weeks on Reddit viewing r/PrintSF and r/Fantasy and notices:

- Members frequently request "character-driven sci-fi" and "hopeful futures, not dystopias"
- They love discussing world-building complexity and

scientific accuracy
- They engage heavily with posts about lesser-known authors and underrated books
- They recommend books using phrases like "thoughtful exploration" and "optimistic without being naive"
- Popular content: deep-dive discussions, comp requests ("books like X but with Y"), reading challenges

She refines her persona: Her readers value intellectual depth, want hopeful narratives, engage with analytical content, and actively seek new authors in their niche.

Nonfiction example: An organizational change consultant observes nonprofit leadership forums and notices:

- Leaders repeatedly mention "doing more with less" and "mission vs. sustainability"
- They're frustrated by advice about limited corporate budgets and hierarchical structures
- They value "mission-driven approaches" that honor nonprofit culture
- They seek "practical tools we can actually implement" not "inspirational vision"
- Popular content: case studies from other nonprofits, tactical how-tos, peer problem-solving

He refines his persona: His readers are resource-constrained, values-driven leaders who need tactical guidance that respects nonprofit context.

Step 4: Identify Platform Habits (15 minutes)

Based on Steps 2-3, where do your readers spend time online?

For each persona, identify:

- Primary platform (where they spend most time)
- Secondary platform (where they also engage)
- Content types they respond to (articles, videos, quick tips, deep dives, visual posts)
- Communities they participate in (specific groups, communities, subreddits)

Fiction example:

- Persona Maria (romance reader, 42): Primary platform is Goodreads romance groups, secondary is romance-focused Facebook groups. Engages with: book recommendations, trope discussions, author Q&As. Discovers books through: Goodreads lists, group recommendations, romance blogs.

Nonfiction example:

- Persona Alex (nonprofit leader, 39): Primary platform is LinkedIn, secondary is nonprofit leadership forums. Engages with: tactical how-to posts, case studies, peer discussions. Discovers books through: LinkedIn recommendations, professional development networks, nonprofit conferences.

This tells you exactly where to focus your content creation efforts.

Step 5: Create Your 2-3 Reader Persona Profiles (30 minutes)

Now synthesize what you've learned into 2-3 detailed personas. Give them names—it makes them real and helps you create content for actual people, not abstractions.

Start with your PRIMARY persona—the reader most likely to love your work and become a loyal advocate.

Template:

PERSONA NAME: [Choose a name]

Age & Life Stage: [Be specific: "43, director-level, teenagers at home" not "35-50"]

Occupation (if relevant): [Helps you understand their context and constraints]

Reading Motivation: [Why do they read books like yours? Escape? Learning? Validation? Processing emotions?]

Emotional Needs: [What feeling are they seeking? Hope? Empowerment? Comfort? Challenge?]

Reading Habits: [When and where do they read? How do they read (ebook, print, audio)?]

Discovery Behavior: [How do they find books? Friends? Goodreads? Podcasts? Algorithms? Bookstores?]

Platform Habits: [Primary and secondary platforms; what content they engage with]

Values/Preferences: [What matters to them in books? What do they seek? What do they avoid?]

Pain Points/Frustrations: [What are they tired of? What gaps do existing books have?]

Language They Use: [5-10 direct quotes from

reviews/communities]

Where to Reach Them: [Specific platforms, communities, groups where they're active]

Content They'll Respond To: [Based on everything above, what topics and formats resonate?]

Example - Fiction Persona:

PERSONA NAME: Jen

Age & Life Stage: 46, marketing manager, two college-aged kids, married

Occupation: Corporate marketing (relevant because she values smart, sophisticated narratives)

Reading Motivation: Escape and emotional engagement after demanding days; wants to feel something but needs resolution and hope

Emotional Needs: Encouragement, hope, belief that growth is possible even through difficulty

Reading Habits: 30 minutes before bed (needs to finish feeling settled), weekend mornings; prefers ebook for convenience

Discovery Behavior: Goodreads recommendations from trusted reviewers, book podcast mentions (Currently Reading, What Should I Read Next), indie bookstore newsletters

Platform Habits: Primary: Goodreads (daily browsing, list-making). Secondary: Book-focused Facebook groups (lurks more than posts). Engages with: book recommendations, reading challenges, author Q&As

Values/Preferences: Women's fiction with emotional depth, flawed but striving characters, hope earned through struggle, contemporary settings, completed stories

Pain Points: Tired of predictable plots; wants complexity but not darkness for darkness's sake; frustrated when endings feel unearned

Language She Uses: "emotionally resonant," "complex characters," "hopeful but not naive," "couldn't put it down," "satisfied ending," "real and raw"

Where to Reach Jen: Goodreads groups (Women's Fiction, Book Recommendations), book podcast listener communities, indie bookstore events

Content She'll Respond To: Posts about emotional authenticity in fiction, behind-the-scenes on character development, book recommendations with similar themes, discussions about hope vs. toxic positivity in storytelling

Example - Nonfiction Persona:

PERSONA NAME: Marcus

Age & Life Stage: 39, newly promoted to VP level, no kids, partnered

Occupation: Tech company VP of Product

Reading Motivation: Professional development; needs practical frameworks for navigating executive-level challenges

Emotional Needs: Confidence that he can succeed at this level, validation that the transition is difficult, clarity on next steps

Reading Habits: Lunch breaks (needs digestible chunks), Sunday mornings (deeper reading); mix of ebook and audiobook during workouts

Discovery Behavior: LinkedIn posts and recommendations, peer suggestions from VP-level networks, business podcasts (HBR IdeaCast, Masters of Scale)

Platform Habits: Primary: LinkedIn (daily professional development scrolling). Secondary: Twitter/X for industry news. Engages with: tactical how-tos, case studies, frameworks, peer discussions

Values/Preferences: Evidence-based approaches, real examples from tech contexts, frameworks without jargon, acknowledgment that leadership is hard

Pain Points: Tired of aspirational leadership content; frustrated by advice written for Fortune 500 contexts; needs tech-specific guidance

Language He Uses: "practical and tactical," "no fluff," "useful," "relevant to tech," "honest about challenges"

Where to Reach Marcus: LinkedIn (tech leadership groups, VP networks), tech leadership Slack channels, business podcast listener groups

Content He'll Respond To: Posts about VP-level transitions, navigating executive presence in tech, practical frameworks for product leadership, case studies from tech companies

Create 1-2 secondary personas using the same template. These are readers who also love your work but might differ in age, platform habits, or discovery behavior. Having 2-3 personas ensures you're not too narrow while still maintaining strategic focus.

Putting Your Personas to Work

Once you have your 2-3 reader personas, use them to drive every content and platform decision. If Persona Jen discovers books through Goodreads and book podcasts, focus your energy there—engage in Goodreads groups where she hangs out, pitch the podcasts she listens to for author interviews. If Persona Marcus finds books through LinkedIn and peer networks, create tactical content on LinkedIn and build relationships in VP-level communities.

Your personas tell you what content to create (topics and tone that resonate), where to post it (platforms they use), and what language converts (their own words). Every strategic decision becomes clearer because you're connecting with readers you understand. You become familiar and recognizable by consistently showing up where your readers are with content they care about—which leads to curiosity, book discovery, and sales.

CALIBRATION: Are Your Reader Personas Useful?

A good reader persona helps you make decisions.

Warning Signs:

✖ Your personas are too generic

"Women 30-50 who like historical fiction" doesn't help you make strategic decisions.

Solution: Add psychographics, platform habits, and emotional needs. Be specific enough that you can picture a real person.

✖ Your personas don't help you decide what to post or where

You have detailed profiles, but when faced with "What should I post this week?" you're still stuck.

Solution: Make sure your personas include platform habits, content preferences, and discovery behavior. That's what makes them actionable.

✖ You created personas based on who you WISH was reading

You want literary readers, but your actual readers want faster pacing and genre conventions.

Solution: Trust the data. Build personas based on observable patterns, not aspirations.

✖ You have five personas and can't prioritize

You're trying to serve too many audiences and diluting your efforts.

Solution: Identify your PRIMARY persona. Secondary personas inform decisions, but your primary reader drives strategy.

Good Signs:

✓ **Your personas help you make platform decisions confidently**

"Persona Jen discovers books through Goodreads and podcasts, so I'll focus there instead of TikTok."

✓ **Content creation feels easier**

You're writing to specific people using language they recognize. It feels like a conversation.

✓ **You're attracting readers who match your personas**

The people engaging with your content, joining your list, and buying your books align with your persona profiles.

✓ **Your personas evolve based on real feedback**

As you gather more data, you refine them. They're living tools, not one-time exercises.

✓ **You reference your personas when making decisions**

Before posting content or choosing a platform, you ask: "Would Persona Jen/Marcus respond to this?"

WORKROOM: Build Your Reader Personas

LEVEL 1: ESSENTIAL (Start here) – 30 minutes

Step 1: Initial Observations

Based on reviews or comp title readers who consume books like mine

Age range and life stage:

What they're seeking emotionally:

Where I see them online:

Step 2: Review Mining

Read 20-30 reviews. Pull 5 quotes about:

What readers loved:

1.

2.

3.

Language they use:

1.

2.

3.

Step 3: Quick Primary Persona

Name:

Age & Life Stage:

Why they read books like mine:

Where they discover books:

Primary platform:

What they value most:

LEVEL 2: DEEPER PERSONA BUILDING (1-2 weeks)

Community Observation:

Join one reader community. Spend a week observing. What patterns do you notice?

What content gets the most engagement?

What language appears repeatedly?

Full Primary Persona:

Use the complete template from Step 5 to create your detailed primary persona including all sections.

Secondary Persona(s):

Create 1-2 additional personas for other readers who also love your work but differ in platform habits or discovery behavior.

Action Plan:

Based on my personas:

- I'll focus on these 2 platforms:

- I'll create content about these 3 topics:
- I'll use this language (pulled from personas):

You don't need to understand every reader who might pick up your book. You need to deeply understand your 2-3 ideal readers—the people most likely to love your work, recommend it passionately, and become loyal fans.

When you know them this well, every decision becomes strategic. You're not scattered across platforms hoping something works—you're showing up where your readers are, with content they want, building familiarity that leads to curiosity, discovery, and sales.

You've defined who you are (ME Factor), what you promise emotionally (Emotional Promise), where you fit competitively (Market Intelligence), and now who you're writing for (Reader Personas). This foundation—identity, positioning, market understanding, and audience clarity—makes everything that follows work to your advantage.

In Chapter 6, we'll explore market gaps and category strategy—understanding not just where you fit, but where the opportunities are that your work can uniquely fill.

You're building something that will last – one strategic decision at a time.

CHAPTER 6

MARKET GAPS: FINDING YOUR WHITE SPACE

The readers who will love your book are already looking for it—they just don't know it exists yet.

They're scrolling through Amazon categories, feeling frustrated. They're asking bookstore staff for recommendations that don't quite exist. They're in book club meetings saying, "I wish someone would write a book about..." They're searching TikTok and Instagram posts describing the exact experience your book delivers—but they can't find you.

Not because your book isn't good enough. Because you haven't positioned it where they're searching.

WHAT: Market Gaps and Category Positioning

A market gap isn't about writing to trend or chasing what's hot. It's about discovering where your authentic work intersects with unmet reader demand.

Think of it this way: readers have appetites that aren't being fully satisfied. Maybe they love cozy mysteries but wish more featured diverse protagonists. Maybe they're hungry for business books about leadership transitions specifically for women in tech. Maybe they adore fantasy with complex political intrigue but want stories set outside medieval European settings.

These gaps exist everywhere. And when your authentic work fills one of these gaps—when what you naturally write meets what readers actively want—that's when your visibility sees exponential growth.

Category strategy is the practical application of gap analysis. It's how you position your book within Amazon's discovery system (and by extension, how bookstores and libraries classify you) so that readers searching for exactly what you offer can find you.

Here's what category strategy is NOT:

- Abandoning your authentic voice to fit a trending niche
- Writing "to market" in a way that compromises your creative vision
- Choosing categories based solely on competition level

Here's what it IS:

- Understanding where readers who will love your work are actively searching
- Positioning your book where demand exceeds supply
- Making strategic choices about how you describe and classify your work
- Finding the sweet spot between specificity and reach

When authors say, "my book doesn't fit neatly into one category," they often mean it as a limitation. But it's an opportunity. Books that live at the intersection of multiple reader interests can claim white space that single-category books can't access.

Your job isn't to contort your work into an ill-fitting box. Your job is to identify which boxes your work authentically belongs in—and then choose the ones where readers are actively searching but supply hasn't caught up with demand.

WHY: Niche Positioning Beats Broad Appeal

The Data: The math of book discovery defies common sense, rewarding specificity in ways that feel backward to authors trained to seek the widest possible audience. Amazon's ranking system reveals a stark advantage for niche positioning: books need only 3-5 daily sales to hit #1 in certain targeted subcategories, while broad, competitive categories require 90+ daily sales for the same ranking. Finding your white space can deliver better visibility.

What does this mean? A #1 bestseller in a targeted niche and a book ranked #100,000 overall sell roughly the same number of daily copies. But here's the crucial difference: the niche bestseller is visible, discoverable, and building momentum with exactly its right readers. The broadly ranked book gets lost in the overall marketplace noise.

This is the paradox of modern publishing: narrower positioning often leads to broader success.

For Business Authors: The Riches in Niches Principle

If you've spent time in business strategy, you already know this concept. A company trying to be everything to everyone captures no one's passionate loyalty. But a company that serves a specific customer segment exceptionally well? They dominate that segment, build fierce advocacy, and eventually expand from that strong foundation.

Your book works the same way. A leadership book trying to serve all leaders gets lost among thousands of generic leadership titles. A leadership book specifically for mid-career women transitioning from individual contributor to people manager in tech companies? That's a specific reader with a specific need, actively searching for exactly that guidance.

You're not limiting your audience—you're claiming the readers most likely to love your work.

For Fiction Authors: Genre-Bending as Strategic Advantage

A secret advantage for fiction authors: That fantasy novel with a strong romantic subplot? It can claim white space in both epic fantasy AND romantasy categories. That legal thriller with political corruption? It speaks to both courtroom drama readers AND political thriller fans.

The key is understanding which combinations are actively sought by readers. Historical romance with mystery elements has an established appetite—readers love both the romantic arc and the puzzle. But romance readers won't embrace ambiguous literary endings – they need their HEAs (happily ever afters). When genre expectations conflict rather than complement, positioning becomes harder.

Your genre-blending isn't a bug—it's a feature, IF you position it where readers with those specific blended appetites are searching.

The Visibility Amplification Effect

When you claim the right niche, three things happen simultaneously:

First, you become discoverable. Readers searching for exactly what you offer find you in their search results, category browsing, and "readers also bought" recommendations.

Second, you become memorable. When you're the only author —or one of a few—serving a specific reader appetite, readers remember you. 'Oh, that's the book about X for Y readers' becomes your calling card.

Third, you become promotable. Bookstores, libraries, book clubs, and media outlets are always looking for specific books to recommend for specific needs. "Do you have any books about [specific thing]?" If you're positioned clearly, you're the answer.

This grows over time. Early readers find you, follow you, and create the word-of-mouth recommendations that bring wider audiences. But it starts with claiming a specific position.

The Fear of Being Too Narrow

Most authors worry that niche positioning will limit their readership. The opposite is true.

Think about breakout books in the past decade. *The Martian* was "hard science fiction survival story with humor"—incredibly specific. *Educated* was "memoir about religious extremism and self-education"—very narrow. *Where the Crawdads Sing* was "coming-of-age murder mystery set in Southern marshlands"—highly particular.

None of these authors started by trying to write for "everyone who likes fiction" or "everyone interested in memoirs." They claimed specific white space, built passionate early readership, and expanded from there.

Broad appeal is the result of narrow positioning done well. Not the strategy itself.

HOW: Finding and Claiming Your White Space

Now let's get practical. How do you identify gaps and position strategically?

Step 1: Map Your Competitive Landscape (With Fresh Eyes)

You did market intelligence work in Chapter 4, identifying comp titles and noticing patterns. Now you're going to look at that same landscape differently—not for what's similar, but for what's missing.

Go back to your list of 8-10 comp titles. As you review them, ask:

- What do readers consistently wish these books included?
- What reader complaints appear in 3-star reviews across multiple comp titles?
- What elements do readers mention wanting more of?
- What reader groups are mentioned in reviews as "this book wasn't for me, but if you're [X type of reader], you'd love it"?

Those 3-star reviews are gold. They're readers saying, "I wanted to love this, but..." or "This was good, but I really wished..." They're articulating unmet needs and that's data that you can use.

Fiction example: You're writing contemporary romance. Your comp titles' reviews keep mentioning "I wish there was more conflict beyond just miscommunication" and "I wanted the characters to have real careers, not just vague creative jobs." That's a gap. Romance with substantive external conflict and characters in clearly defined professional roles has appetite.

Nonfiction example: You're writing about productivity for creative professionals. Comp titles' reviews mention "too many corporate examples, not enough for freelancers" and "great systems but unrealistic for people with ADHD." That's your white space: productivity books for neurodivergent creative freelancers.

Step 2: Mine Amazon Categories for Demand Signals

Amazon's category system is imperfect, but it reveals what readers are actively searching for. Your goal: find categories where reader demand exceeds book supply.

Here's how to assess a category's viability:

Browse Amazon's category structure (not just searching but click through Categories > Books > [Your Genre] and explore subcategories). Look for categories where:

- The #1 bestseller has a rank better than #50,000 overall (meaning there's active buying)
- The #10 bestseller has a rank worse than #100,000 overall (meaning supply is limited)
- Books on the first page show recent publication dates (meaning it's not dominated by classics)

This sweet spot—strong demand at #1, weak supply by #10—is where you want to position.

Pay attention to category names themselves. Amazon creates categories in response to reader search behavior. If a category exists, readers are searching for it. Categories like "African American Science Fiction," "Women Sleuths Mystery," or "Organizational Change Management" exist because those specific combinations are being sought.

For your book, identify 3-5 categories that authentically fit your work AND show that demand-exceeds-supply pattern.

Step 3: Test Category Positioning with Your Reader Personas

Remember Personas Jen and Marcus? Now they're going to help you reality-test your category choices.

For each category you're considering, ask:

- Would [Persona Name] search or browse this category?
- Does this category use language [Persona Name] would use to describe what they're looking for?
- If [Persona Name] browsed this category, would they expect to find books like mine?

If the answer is no to any of these, the category might technically fit but might not help those specific readers discover you.

Example: You write a business book about organizational change using narrative storytelling. "Business > Management" is technically accurate, but your mid-level manager readers also browse "Business > Leadership" and "Self-Help > Personal Transformation." Choose categories where your readers look, not just where your book technically fits.

Step 4: Identify Your Specific Competitive Advantage Within the Gap

This is where the ME Factor from Chapter 2 becomes crucial. You've identified a gap—now, how does YOUR specific approach fill it in a way that's different from the few books that do exist in this space?

Go back to your ME Factor formula: Goal + Audience + YOU.

Let's say you've identified a gap: business books about leadership for first-time managers in healthcare settings. Great —but what's YOUR specific angle?

Maybe your YOU factor is "former ER nurse who became a

hospital administrator." That's differentiation within the gap. You're not just writing for healthcare managers—you're writing for healthcare managers with clinical backgrounds who are transitioning to administrative roles. That's more specific than the gap itself.

For fiction: You've identified a gap for historical fantasy set in non-European cultures. Your YOU factor might be "fantasy writer with academic background in West African history." You're not just filling the historical fantasy gap—you're filling it with specific cultural expertise and perspective that creates further differentiation.

Your competitive advantage isn't just "I write in the gap." It's "I fill this gap in a way that only I can, because of my specific combination of experience, perspective, and approach."

Step 5: Craft Your Category Strategy Statement

Now synthesize everything into a clear positioning statement. This isn't for public marketing—this is for your own strategic clarity.

Your Category Strategy Statement: "My book positions at the intersection of [Category 1] and [Category 2], serving [Primary Reader Persona] who wants [specific unmet need]. My competitive advantage in this white space is [your unique ME factor]. I will claim visibility in these 3-5 Amazon categories: [list them]."

Fiction example:

"My book sits at the intersection of psychological suspense and women's fiction, serving Persona Jen who wants character-driven mysteries with unreliable narrators and domestic settings. My competitive advantage is prose quality and emotional depth beyond typical thrillers. I will claim visibility in: Psychological Thrillers, Domestic Thrillers, Literary Suspense, Women's Fiction (Contemporary), and Psychological Fiction."

Nonfiction example:

"My book positions at the intersection of career development and workplace psychology, serving Persona Marcus who wants practical guidance for navigating organizational politics without compromising integrity. My competitive advantage is frameworks from both psychology research and 15 years as an executive coach. I will claim visibility in: Business Mentoring & Coaching, Workplace Culture, Career Success, Business Conflict Resolution, and Organizational Behavior."

This statement becomes your North Star for all positioning decisions—from your book description to how you pitch to bookstores to what content you create.

CALIBRATION: Are You Positioned in the Right Niche?

Here's how to know if your category strategy is working—or needs adjustment.

Warning Signs Your Positioning Needs Work:

✗ **You struggle to explain who your book is for in one sentence.** If it takes you a full paragraph of "Well, it's kind of like X, but also Y, and there's some Z..." your positioning is too diffuse. If you can't articulate it clearly, readers can't either. (And that's okay—Chapter 2 on the ME Factor will help you clarify this.)

❌ **Your comp titles span wildly different categories with no overlap.** If your comp titles include a literary novel, a thriller, and a self-help book, you haven't identified your actual competitive set. You've identified books you personally like, not books readers would compare yours to. (If you need help identifying true comps, revisit Chapter 4.)

❌ **The categories you're considering have either no competition or thousands of books.** No competition often means no reader demand. Thousands of books means you'll be invisible. You want the Goldilocks zone: active demand, manageable supply. (If you're unsure how to assess this, the Workroom exercise below will walk you through it step by step.)

❌ **Your reader personas wouldn't naturally browse your chosen categories.** If persona Jen wouldn't think to look in "Business Technology" for your tech thriller, that category won't help her find you, even if it's technically accurate.

❌ **You're choosing categories based on ranking potential, not reader fit.** If you're thinking "I could hit #1 in this obscure category" but the category doesn't authentically describe your book, you're gaming the system, not positioning strategically. This also runs the risk of disappointing readers if your book is marketed incorrectly.

Good Signs Your Positioning Is Working:

✔ **You can describe your niche in a single, specific sentence.** "I write international thrillers for readers who want complex, high impact plots in global settings." Clear, specific, authentic. If you can say it this cleanly, readers can understand it too.

✔ **Your categories share 2-3 comp titles in their top 20 bestsellers.** This means you've identified categories that genuinely overlap—where the same readers browse multiple category spaces looking for books like yours.

✔ **Readers describe your book using the same language you use to position it.** When early readers, reviewers, or book club members say, "This is perfect for people who want [exact thing you identified]," you've nailed the positioning.

✔ **Your chosen categories show active buying (#1 ranks around #50,000 or better) but aren't dominated by backlist classics.** This means readers are buying books in this niche, and newer authors can gain visibility there.

✔ **You feel excited, not constrained, by your positioning.** The right niche feels like permission to be exactly who you are, not a box that limits you. If your category strategy makes you think "Yes! These are MY readers!" you've found your white space.

✔ **You can point to at least one unmet reader need your book addresses.** Based on comp title reviews or reader community conversations, you know what gap you're filling. You're not just another book in the category—you're answering a question that hasn't been fully answered yet.

This book will teach you every single one of these skills—from clarifying your ME Factor to identifying true comps to building reader personas. If you notice warning signs, the referenced chapters will help you build the foundation you need. And you'll come back to this chapter with fresh clarity.

WORKROOM: Gap Analysis & Category Selection

LEVEL 1: ESSENTIAL (Start here) – 30 minutes

Quick Gap Discovery:

1. Pull up your 3-5 top comp titles from Chapter 4 (the books most similar to yours in approach and audience)
2. Read twenty 3-star reviews across these titles (4 per book)
3. Make a list: What do readers consistently say they wished the books included? What complaints appear multiple times?
4. Circle the 2-3 most frequently mentioned unmet needs
5. Ask yourself: Does my book address any of these needs? If yes, that's your gap positioning angle

Basic Category Selection:

1. Go to Amazon > Books > Your Primary Genre
2. Browse subcategories (don't search—click through the category tree)
3. Identify 3 categories where: (a) your book authentically fits, and (b) the #1 book ranks around #50,000 or better overall
4. Check: Would your Primary Reader Persona from Chapter 5 naturally browse these categories?
5. Write down your top 3 category choices

That's your foundation. You now know what gap you might fill and where to position. Everything else builds from here.

LEVEL 2: IF YOU WANT TO GO DEEPER (Optional)

Extended Gap Analysis:

- Read ten 3-star reviews across your full list of comp titles from Chapter 4
- Track unmet needs in a simple document: What readers wished for | How often mentioned | Does my book address this?
- Look for patterns across different reviewer types (note: some readers wanted more romance, others wanted less —that's a positioning insight about different reader segments)
- Browse one Goodreads group related to your genre and notice what readers ask for in recommendation threads
- Synthesize: What's the most significant unmet need that your book authentically addresses?

Category Deep Dive:

- Explore 5 potential categories (not just your initial 3)
- For each category, check the ranks of books at positions #1, #10, and #20
- Note: Are recent releases ranking well, or is it dominated by backlist?
- Identify categories where you see other books with similar positioning (genre-blending, specific niche, etc.) succeeding
- Select your top 5 categories with a one-sentence rationale for each

Persona-Category Alignment:

- Take your 2-3 reader personas from Chapter 5
- For each persona, jot down: What would they search for on Amazon? What language would they use?
- Test your category selections: Would each persona

naturally land in these categories?
- Adjust category choices based on persona browsing behavior, not just technical fit

LEVEL 3: DEEP DIVE (Come back to this over weeks/months)

Comprehensive Market Mapping:

Create a visual map of your competitive landscape:

- List 6-7 books in your broader market space
- Plot them on two axes: Specific to Broad (positioning) and High Visibility to Low Visibility (sales rank)
- Notice: Where are the clusters? Where are the gaps? Where do highly specific books succeed?
- Identify the white space where your book could claim territory
- Write a brief analysis: This is my unique positioning within the larger landscape because...

Category Testing Strategy:

Before publication:

- Identify 5-7 potential categories
- Research each: top 20 books, typical ranks
- Select your initial 5 categories based on strategic fit
- Plan to test different category combinations post-launch
- Document your hypothesis: "I believe Category X will work because..."

After publication (or for already-published books):

- Check monthly: Your rank in each category, visibility

in "also bought" recommendations
- Test category changes quarterly: Swap one category, measure impact over 30 days
- Monitor which categories drive discovery with your strongest comp titles
- Refine strategy based on actual performance data

Reader Language Research:

This is market intelligence gold:

- Join 1-2 online reader communities related to your genre/topic (Facebook groups, LinkedIn groups, Goodreads groups, Reddit communities)
- Spend one week observing: What language do readers use to describe what they're looking for? What books do they recommend? What gaps do they articulate?
- Create a simple document of reader language: common phrases, frequent requests, how they describe books vs. how the industry describes them
- Use this language in your category strategy, book description, and positioning

Competitive Advantage Summary:

Create a quick comparison of 5-6 books closest to your niche:

- For each book, note: Primary strength | Primary weakness (based on reviews) | How yours is different
- Synthesize into one clear statement: "My competitive advantage in this niche is [specific differentiation] because [your unique background/approach/perspective]"
- Use this when pitching to media or bookstores

One-Paragraph Positioning Summary:

Write a single paragraph that synthesizes your strategic positioning. Use this template:

"My book [TITLE] positions at the intersection of [CATEGORY 1] and [CATEGORY 2], serving [PRIMARY READER PERSONA NAME] who wants [SPECIFIC UNMET NEED]. My competitive advantage is [YOUR UNIQUE YOU FACTOR from Chapter 2]. I claim visibility in these Amazon categories: [LIST 3-5 CATEGORIES]. This positioning is authentic to my work because [ONE SENTENCE about why this fits who you are and what you write]."

This becomes your quick reference for all positioning decisions. When you're unsure about a marketing opportunity, ask: Does this serve my positioning, or dilute it?

The readers who will love your book are already looking for it. Your job is to position it where they're searching—clearly, strategically, and authentically. Not by contorting your work into an ill-fitting category, but by identifying the white space your work naturally occupies and claiming it with intention.

This is not gaming the system. It's strategic positioning. And it's how visibility magnifies over time.

PART III

THE STRATEGY: BUILDING YOUR AUTHOR BRAND

This is the bridge where Identity meets Market Intelligence. Your brand is the integration of who you are, where you fit, and who you serve.

For debut authors: This section translates everything you've learned into a cohesive brand system—complete with content pillars that make marketing manageable instead of overwhelming.

For published authors: This section exposes brand drift—the misalignment between who you are, what you promise, and how you show up. You'll create consistency that makes you recognizable and memorable to readers.

For returning authors: This section helps you synthesize your past work with your current vision into a unified brand. You're not starting over—you're building on what already exists with strategic intention.

CHAPTER 7

AUTHOR BRANDING: WHERE IT ALL COMES TOGETHER

Your author brand isn't what you say about yourself—it's the promise readers can count on.

Think about the authors whose books you buy without reading the description first. You know their name, their genre, their brand and their emotional promise. You know what you're getting, not because every book is identical, but because there's a consistent experience you trust. That's author branding working exactly as it should.

Here's what authors often misunderstand about branding: they think it means creating a public persona separate from their private self. The "author version" of who they are. The professional mask.

That's not branding. It's a type of performance that demands constant effort.

Your author brand isn't a carefully curated image you maintain. It's the consistent truth of who you are, expressed across every reader touchpoint. It's what happens when your ME Factor, your emotional promise, your market positioning, and your actual personality converge.

The strongest author brands aren't the most polished. They're the most coherent. When readers visit your website, scroll your social media, read your newsletter, and hear you speak at an event, they should encounter the same person—not because you're performing consistently, but because you're being true to who you are.

This is why the ME Factor matters. It's not about what you think readers want. It's about what you can deliver authentically, repeatedly, without burning out or losing yourself in the process.

Your brand is your promise. And the only promise you can keep long-term is the one rooted in truth.

Your *author brand* is the synthesis of everything you've worked on in the previous chapters. It's where your ME Factor (Chapter 2), your Emotional Promise (Chapter 3), your market intelligence (Chapter 4), your reader personas (Chapter 5), and your category positioning (Chapter 6) align to form something coherent and recognizable.

It's not another thing to create. It's what naturally emerges when you bring strategic clarity to who you are, what you write, and who you write for.

WHAT: Author Branding as Strategic Synthesis

Your author brand is the reliable, recognizable experience readers associate with your name.

It's not your bio. It's not your social media aesthetic. It's not your author photo or your website design. Those are expressions of your brand, but they're not the brand itself.

Your brand is the consistent through-line that connects:

- What you write about (your ME Factor)
- How you make readers feel (your Emotional Promise)
- Where you fit in the market (your positioning)
- Who your work serves (your readers)

When these elements combine, something powerful happens: readers know what to expect from you. Not in an "every book is the same" way, but in a trust-building "I know this author gets me" way.

Here's the difference between an author with a clear brand and one without:

Without a clear brand: A reader picks up your book, loves it, and thinks "That was great!" But when they try to recommend it to a friend, they struggle to articulate what makes your work distinctive. When your next book comes out, they don't immediately think "I need to read that" because they're not sure what to expect.

With a clear brand: A reader picks up your book, loves it, and thinks "This is exactly what I needed." When they recommend it, they can clearly articulate what makes your work special and who else would love it. When your next book comes out, they think "Yes, I know I'll love this" because they trust the consistent experience you deliver.

Your author brand makes you memorable, recommendable, and trustworthy. It's not about boxing yourself in—it's about giving readers a reason to come back.

WHY: Brand Clarity Expands Over Time

The Data: Authors with established personal brands and engaged audiences see 2-5x higher first-week sales compared to authors without a strong brand presence. And we've already established that readers who have enjoyed 2 or more of your books in the past are likely to buy your next book. Why? Because they know your voice and they trust your emotional promise.

But here's the catch: this only works when there's a recognizable through-line across your work. If every book feels completely random, readers can't build that trust. They might love individual books, but they won't become invested in YOU as an author.

When readers know what to expect from you—and that expectation is consistently met—they become loyal buyers who show up for every single release. They don't need to be convinced. They're already sold.

For Business Authors: Your Brand is Your Authority Platform

If you're writing business or leadership books, your author brand is inseparable from your professional credibility. Readers aren't just buying a book—they're buying into your expertise and perspective.

A clear author brand answers these questions before readers even open your book:

- What is this author's specific area of expertise?
- What perspective or approach do they bring that's different?
- Will this author's way of thinking resonate with how I see the world?

Think about business authors you trust: Brené Brown brings vulnerability research to leadership. Adam Grant brings organizational psychology to work culture. Patrick Lencioni brings narrative storytelling to business strategy. Their brands aren't just topics—they're specific lenses through which they view their topics.

Your author brand is your consistent lens. It's what makes readers think "I want to hear what [your name] has to say about this topic" rather than just "I want to read about this topic."

For Fiction Authors: Your Brand Builds Reader Trust

Fiction readers are taking a risk every time they pick up a new book. Will they love it? Will it disappoint them? Will it be worth their time and emotional investment?

Your author brand reduces that risk. It tells readers: "If you loved my last book, you'll love this one too, even though the plot and characters are completely different."

That's not about writing the same book over and over. It's about delivering a consistent emotional experience, tone, or thematic focus that readers can count on.

Think about fiction authors with strong brands:

- Readers know a Celeste Ng novel will explore complex family dynamics with nuanced, morally ambiguous characters
- Readers know a Taylor Jenkins Reid book will feature compelling characters facing high-stakes emotional choices, often set against glamorous backdrops
- Readers know a Fredrik Backman book will blend humor and heartbreak in stories about ordinary people in small communities

These authors write different stories every time, but their brand promise remains consistent. That's what lets readers trust them book after book.

HOW: Building Your Author Brand from Strategic Foundations

You've already done most of the work. Now you're going to synthesize it into a clear, consistent brand.

Step 1: Identify Your Brand Through-Line

Go back to the work you did in Chapters 2, 3, and 5:

- Your ME Factor formula (Goal + Audience + YOU)
- Your Emotional Promise (the consistent feeling readers get from your work)
- Your Primary Reader Persona (who your work serves

most directly)

Now ask yourself: What's the connecting thread? What's the one thing readers can always count on from your work?

This isn't about finding a clever tagline. It's about identifying the genuine consistency that already exists across your work.

Fiction example: You write science fiction. Your ME Factor is "exploring what it means to be human through first contact scenarios." Your Emotional Promise is "wonder mixed with existential questioning." Your Primary Reader Persona is someone who loves cerebral sci-fi with strong character development. Your brand through-line might be: "Thoughtful science fiction that explores humanity through alien perspectives."

Nonfiction example: You write about productivity. Your ME Factor is "helping creative professionals build smart systems without sacrificing creativity." Your Emotional Promise is "relief—permission to work differently." Your Primary Reader Persona is a creative freelancer who's tried every productivity system and felt like they all failed. Your brand through-line might be: "Productivity approaches designed for creative, non-linear thinkers."

Your brand through-line should feel true to who you are and what you write. If it feels forced or artificial, keep refining until it clicks.

Step 2: Define Your Brand Expression Elements

Now that you know your brand through-line, you need to define how that brand shows up consistently across everything you create.

Brand expression includes:

- **Voice and tone:** Are you conversational or formal? Humorous or serious? Warm or direct?
- **Visual aesthetic:** What colors, fonts, and imagery reflect your brand? (This doesn't have to be fancy—just consistent.)
- **Content themes:** What topics do you talk about that connect to your brand? What do you NOT talk about because it doesn't serve your brand?
- **Platform presence:** Where do your readers spend time? Where should you show up consistently?

You don't need to define all of this in exhaustive detail right now. But you should be able to answer these questions:

1. If someone read three pieces of content from me (blog posts, social media, newsletter), would they recognize the consistent voice and perspective?
2. Does my visual presence (website, social media, book covers if you have them) feel cohesive?
3. Am I talking about things that connect to what I write, or are my topics haphazard?

Fiction example: You write psychological suspense. Your brand voice is "smart, unsettling, invites readers to question what they think they know." Your visual aesthetic uses dark, moody colors. Your content themes include unreliable narrators, the psychology of deception, and morally complex characters. You focus on Instagram (visual storytelling) and Threads (short, thought-provoking observations). You DON'T post about your personal life or unrelated topics that dilute your brand.

Nonfiction example: You write about organizational culture.

Your brand voice is "pragmatic, empathetic, translates research into real-world application." Your visual aesthetic is clean and professional with warm accent colors. Your content themes include workplace psychology, leadership challenges, and practical frameworks. You focus on LinkedIn (professional audience) and a newsletter (deeper dives). You DON'T post motivational quotes or generic business advice that doesn't connect to your specific expertise.

The goal isn't perfection. The goal is consistency. Readers should be able to recognize your brand across different touchpoints.

Step 3: Create Your Brand Filter

This is the most practical tool you'll develop: a simple set of questions you ask before making any marketing or visibility decision.

Your brand filter helps you decide:

- Should I pursue this speaking opportunity?
- Should I guest post on this blog?
- Should I be on this social media platform?
- Should I write about this topic?
- Should I collaborate with this person or organization?

Here's how to create your brand filter. For any opportunity or decision, ask:

1. **Does this serve my Primary Reader Persona?** If it puts you in front of your target readers, it passes. If it's a random audience, it fails.
2. **Does this align with my brand through-line?** If it reinforces what readers can expect from you, it passes.

If it confuses your positioning, it fails.

3. **Does this feel authentic to who I am?** If you'd do this even without a marketing benefit, it passes. If it feels performative or forced, it fails.

If an opportunity gets three "pass" answers, it's probably worth pursuing. If it gets two or fewer, it's probably not strategic for your brand—even if it seems like a good opportunity.

Example: You're invited to speak at a conference. Your brand is "science fiction exploring AI ethics for readers who want thoughtful, character-driven stories."

- Does this serve my Primary Reader Persona? (Conference is for sci-fi readers who love cerebral stories = YES)
- Does this align with my brand through-line? (Topic is "Ethics in Science Fiction" = YES)
- Does this feel authentic to who I am? (You genuinely care about AI ethics and would enjoy this conversation = YES)

Counter-example: You're invited to guest post on a popular book blog. Your brand is "productivity for creative freelancers."

- Does this serve my Primary Reader Persona? (Blog audience is general fiction readers, not freelancers = NO)
- Does this align with my brand through-line? (Topic would be "writing productivity," which is tangential = MAYBE)
- Does this feel authentic to who I am? (You'd have to write about fiction writing, which isn't your expertise = NO)

Your brand filter protects you from "shiny object syndrome"—chasing every opportunity without asking if it serves your strategic positioning.

Step 4: Document Your Author Brand

Finally, write down your author brand in one clear document. This isn't for public consumption—it's your internal reference.

Your Author Brand Document should include:

Brand Through-Line: [One sentence that captures the consistent experience readers get from your work]

Primary Reader Persona: [Brief description of who your work serves—reference Chapter 5]

Emotional Promise: [The feeling readers can count on—reference Chapter 3]

Category Positioning: [Where you claim white space—reference Chapter 6]

Voice & Tone: [2-3 words that describe how you communicate]

Content Themes: [3 topics you talk about that connect to your brand]

Platform Focus: [1-2 platforms where your readers show up]

Brand Filter Questions: [Your 3 questions for evaluating opportunities]

Example:

Brand Through-Line: Women's fiction exploring emotional resilience and family dynamics through character-driven stories in contemporary settings

Primary Reader Persona: Persona Jen—age 46, marketing manager, reads women's fiction for emotional authenticity and character-driven stories

Emotional Promise: Emotional connection—readers see themselves in authentic characters navigating real-life challenges

Category Positioning: Women's Fiction (Contemporary), Literary Fiction, Domestic Fiction, Family Life Fiction

Voice & Tone: Warm, honest, emotionally intelligent

Content Themes: Character development, emotional authenticity, family relationships, navigating life transitions, women's experiences

Platform Focus: Instagram (visual storytelling), Threads (short observations), newsletter (deeper character explorations)

Brand Filter Questions:

1. Does this serve Persona Jen?
2. Does this align with women's fiction/emotional authenticity blend?
3. Does this feel authentic to my interest in family dynamics and character?

This document becomes your touchstone for every visibility

decision. When you're unsure about whether to pursue an opportunity, deciding what content to create, or feeling unsure of your creative direction, come back to this document.

Your author brand isn't one more thing to manage. It's the element that makes everything else work.

CALIBRATION: Is Your Brand Working?

Here's how to know if your author brand is clear and consistent —or needs refinement.

Warning Signs Your Brand Needs Clarity:

✗   **People describe your work differently every time.** If early readers, reviewers, or colleagues can't consistently articulate what your work is about or who it's for, your brand isn't clear yet. (And that's okay—revisit your ME Factor in Chapter 2 and your Emotional Promise in Chapter 3. Those are your brand foundations.)

✗ **You feel scattered across different platforms and topics.** If you're talking about productivity on Monday, travel on Wednesday, and your writing process on Friday, with no connecting thread, your brand expression is too diffuse. (Chapter 8 on Content Pillars will help you focus this.)

✗ **You pursue every opportunity that comes your way.** If you say yes to speaking gigs, guest posts, and collaborations without a strategic filter, you're building visibility without building brand recognition. Scattered visibility doesn't grow your brand.

✗   **Your visual presence feels random.** If your website, social media, and marketing materials look like they're for three different authors, readers can't form a coherent impression of your brand. (You don't need to hire a designer—you just need consistency.)

✖ **You're not sure what to post or talk about.** If you stare at a blank social media post or newsletter wondering "what should I say?" every time, you haven't defined your content themes clearly enough. Your brand should make content creation easier, not harder.

Good Signs Your Brand Is Working:

✔ **People can describe your books in one clear sentence.** When readers, reviewers, or colleagues say "Oh, you write [specific thing] for [specific readers]" without hesitation, your brand is landing. They get it.

✔ **New readers find you through consistent recommendations.** When people discover you because someone said, "If you like [X], you'll love this author," that's brand clarity creating word-of-mouth. Your through-line is recognizable.

✔ **Content creation feels easier, not harder.** When you know exactly what topics fit your brand and what doesn't, deciding what to post or write about becomes straightforward. You're not reinventing the wheel every time.

✔ **You can quickly evaluate opportunities.** When someone offers you a speaking gig, guest post, or collaboration, you can immediately assess whether it serves your brand or dilutes it. Decision-making becomes faster and more confident.

✔ **Your marketing feels authentic, not performative.** When showing up on social media, sending newsletters, or engaging with readers feels like a natural extension of who you are (not a chore you're forcing yourself to do), your brand is aligned with your authentic identity.

✔ **Readers describe your books using the same language you use.** When reviews, recommendations, and reader conversations reflect the same themes, tone, and positioning you've identified in your brand, you've successfully communicated your through-line. Your brand isn't just in your head—it's reaching readers.

This book will teach you every single one of these skills—from defining your ME Factor to crafting content themes to making strategic platform choices. You don't need to have it all figured out yet. If you notice warning signs, the referenced chapters will help you build the clarity you need. And you'll return to this chapter with much stronger foundations.

WORKROOM: Building Your Author Brand Document

LEVEL 1: ESSENTIAL (Start here) – 30 minutes

Quick Brand Synthesis:

1. Pull out your work from previous chapters:
    o Your ME Factor from Chapter 2
    o Your Emotional Promise from Chapter 3
    o Your Primary Reader Persona from Chapter 5
2. Write one sentence that captures your brand through-line by filling in this template: "I write [genre/topic] that [what makes it distinctive] for [who it serves]."
3. List 2-3 topics you could talk about that connect

directly to your brand through-line (not random topics —things that reinforce what readers can expect from you)

4. Answer this question: If someone could only know ONE thing about what makes my work distinctive, what would it be?

That's your foundation. You now have a clear brand through-line and starting point for consistent messaging.

LEVEL 2: IF YOU WANT TO GO DEEPER (Optional)

Expanded Brand Definition:

Using the template from the HOW section, create your Author Brand Document:

- Brand Through-Line (one sentence)
- Primary Reader Persona (brief description)
- Emotional Promise (the feeling readers can count on)
- Category Positioning (where you claim white space)
- Voice & Tone (2-3 descriptive words)
- Content Themes (3 topics you'll focus on)
- Platform Focus (1-2 platforms your readers use)

Brand Filter Creation:

Write your three brand filter questions:

1. Does this serve my Primary Reader Persona?
2. Does this align with my brand through-line?
3. Does this feel authentic to who I am?

Test your filter on one opportunity you're currently considering (or a past opportunity you pursued). Run it through your three questions. Would it pass or fail?

LEVEL 3: DEEP DIVE (Come back to this over weeks/months)

Brand Audit:

Look at your current online presence (website, social media profiles, any existing marketing materials):

- Does your visual presence feel cohesive? Are you using consistent colors, fonts, imagery?
- Does your bio or "About" section clearly communicate your brand through-line?
- Do your recent posts reflect your content themes, or are you all over the place?

Make a list of 2-3 things that need to be brought into alignment with your brand. Don't try to fix everything at once—just identify the biggest disconnects.

Content Theme Development:

For each of your 3 content themes, brainstorm 3 specific angles or topics you could create content about:

- Content Theme 1: [3 specific post/article ideas]
- Content Theme 2: [3 specific post/article ideas]
- Content Theme 3: [3 specific post/article ideas]

This gives you a bank of 9 content ideas that all serve your brand. When you're stuck on what to post, reference this list.

Six-Month Brand Consistency Plan:

Choose ONE platform where your Primary Reader Persona spends time. Commit to showing up there consistently for three months with content that reinforces your brand.

Create a simple plan:

- Platform: [Which one?]
- Posting frequency: [How often can you realistically maintain?]
- Content mix: [How will you rotate through your 3 content themes?]
- Brand consistency check: [Once a month, review your posts—do they all reinforce your brand through-line, or are you drifting off-topic?]

This isn't about perfection. It's about using observation, awareness, and intention to build the consistency that lets your brand amplify over time.

Your author brand isn't something you create from scratch. It's something you clarify by bringing strategic focus to who you already are, what you already write, and who you already serve.

When your brand is clear, everything else gets easier. Readers know what to expect. You know what opportunities to pursue. Content creation becomes strategic, not random. And visibility expands because people remember who you are and why you matter.

That's not marketing for marketing's sake. That's strategic protection of your creative work. And it's one of the most valuable things you can build as an author.

CHAPTER 8

CONTENT PILLARS: YOUR STRATEGIC MESSAGING

What if you never had to wonder what to post on social media?

Content pillars make that possible—not through a calendar of random ideas, but through a strategic framework that makes content creation feel natural, aligned, and genuinely useful to your readers. They translate your author brand into strategic messaging that serves both your positioning and your readers' needs.

You've done the hard work of defining who you are (your ME Factor), what readers can count on from you (your emotional promise), where you fit in the market (your positioning), and who your readers are (your personas). Content pillars are how you translate all that strategic clarity into the work of visibility —without posting constantly or second-guessing every decision.

WHAT: Content Pillars as Strategic Framework

Content pillars are the 3-5 core themes or categories that organize all your public-facing content. They're not topics you force yourself to care about because they're "good for marketing"—they emerge naturally from the intersection of your author brand and your readers' needs.

Think of them as the columns supporting your author platform. Each pillar represents a theme you can consistently create content around, and together they create a cohesive brand experience that your target readers—the ones you identified in Chapter 5—will recognize and remember.

Content pillars are NOT:

- A rigid posting schedule that feels like homework
- Topics you think you "should" care about
- Random ideas you saw other authors post about
- A way to talk about your book constantly

Content pillars ARE:

- Strategic themes that reinforce your positioning
- Topics you genuinely care about and can speak to authentically
- A framework that makes content creation manageable
- Tools for building trust before readers ever see your

book

Your content pillars live at the intersection of three things: what you care about, what your readers need, and what reinforces your strategic positioning. When all three align, content creation stops feeling like marketing and becomes a conversation.

WHY: Focused Content Beats Random Posting

Research on brand recognition shows that consistent impressions build memory and familiarity, while random impressions don't always gain traction. When you post randomly—book recommendation today, personal story tomorrow, political comment next week—readers can't form a clear picture of who you are or what you offer. But when your content consistently orbits around your defined pillars, every impression reinforces the last. Readers start to recognize not just your name, but what you stand for.

How do you know content pillars really matter?

The Data: Focused content strategies built around consistent themes generate 30% more engagement and 50% higher click-through rates than scattered, random posting. A *click-through rate* (CTR) measures how often people exposed to your content click on it to learn more. That "click" indicates that your content is compelling enough to inspire curiosity and action. In other words, when you have a focused content strategy instead of posting whatever comes to mind, you become more memorable.

For the fantasy fiction author who writes about chosen

family and belonging:

Imagine seeing an author's social media post about building found family in fiction. Next week, you see that same author share a story about community spaces that foster connection. A few days later, they're discussing how loneliness shapes character motivation. Then they share reader feedback about how their book helped someone feel less alone.

By the fourth impression, you don't just know their name—you know what they care about, you know what kind of stories they tell, and now their consistently-themed content has more meaning. When you're in a bookstore looking at fantasy novels, you'll remember the author who writes about belonging. That's strategic content at work.

For the business author who writes about organizational change:

Another author posts about why top-down change initiatives fail. A week later, they share a case study about frontline employee insights driving innovation. Then they discuss the psychology of resistance to change, and a tool for mapping stakeholder perspectives.

By the time you see their book on organizational leadership, you already know they understand change from the ground up, not from the executive suite. You know their perspective is different. You remember them.

This is why content pillars matter: they create consistent impressions that build recognition and trust. Random posting might keep you visible, but strategic content makes you memorable.

Content pillars solve four common challenges that slow authors down:

1. Decision Fatigue: Without pillars, you face infinite options every time you create content. What should you post? What tone and style will resonate? What type of graphic will catch attention? But with defined pillars, you've already answered those questions. You're choosing between 3-5 themes instead of infinite possibilities.

2. Brand Dilution: When your content spans too many unrelated topics, readers can't figure out who you are or why they should care. Content pillars keep your messaging focused enough to build recognition while still giving you flexibility and creative freedom.

3. Platform Overwhelm: You don't need to be on every platform, and you don't need to post every day. But you DO need consistency. Content pillars make it possible to show up regularly without burning out, because you're working within a strategic framework instead of inventing from scratch every time.

4. Visual Overwhelm: Beyond messaging strategy, there's an execution challenge that stops many authors from posting: every social media post requires an accompanying graphic—this isn't optional. Platforms prioritize visual content, and text-only posts get buried in feeds. But without strategic guidance, creating graphics becomes another time-consuming barrier that keeps authors from posting consistently. You're either spending hours designing visuals or avoiding social media entirely because the visual component feels overwhelming.

HOW: Building Your Content Pillar System

Building content pillars isn't about brainstorming random topics—it's about mining the strategic work you've already done. Your ME Factor, emotional promise, market positioning, and reader personas have already told you what matters. Now you're organizing that clarity into themes you can consistently create content around.

Step 1: Mine Your Strategic Foundation

Start by reviewing the strategic work from earlier chapters:

- Your ME Factor (Goal + Audience + YOU)
- Your emotional promise (the consistent experience readers expect)
- Your reader personas (2-3 profiles with their needs and preferences)
- Your brand through-line (Chapter 7)

Look for recurring themes. What keeps showing up? What do you care about that also matters to your target readers? What reinforces your positioning?

For instance, a fiction author who writes psychological thrillers and whose ME Factor includes "psychological complexity" and whose emotional promise centers on "intellectual stimulation through moral ambiguity" might notice themes emerging around: moral complexity in storytelling, the psychology of decision-making under pressure, and how real-world ethics inform fictional dilemmas.

A nonfiction author who writes about workplace productivity and whose ME Factor includes "sustainable systems for creative professionals" and whose emotional promise is "calm clarity instead of hustle culture" might see themes around: building systems that support creativity (not constrain it), the neuroscience of focus and rest, and rejecting productivity theater.

These aren't random topics—they're the natural extension of who you are and what you offer.

Step 2: Define 3-5 Core Pillars

Most authors need 3-5 content pillars. Fewer than three feels limiting; more than five creates the same decision fatigue you're trying to avoid.

Each pillar should:

- Connect authentically to your interests and expertise
- Matter to your target reader personas
- Reinforce your positioning and emotional promise
- Give you enough scope to create varied content without getting repetitive

Example: Science Fiction Author (Near-Future Climate Fiction)

Let's say you write near-future science fiction exploring climate adaptation. Your ME Factor emphasizes "hope through ingenuity," and your emotional promise is "empowerment, not despair." Your reader personas include environmentally conscious readers, science enthusiasts, and people seeking solutions-oriented narratives.

Your content pillars might be:

1. **Climate Adaptation & Innovation:** Real-world examples of communities and technologies adapting to climate change

2. **Hope in Speculative Fiction:** How science fiction imagines futures beyond dystopia
3. **Science Literacy in Storytelling:** Making complex science accessible and compelling in fiction
4. **Reader Community & Book Recommendations:** Books that inspire action, not paralysis

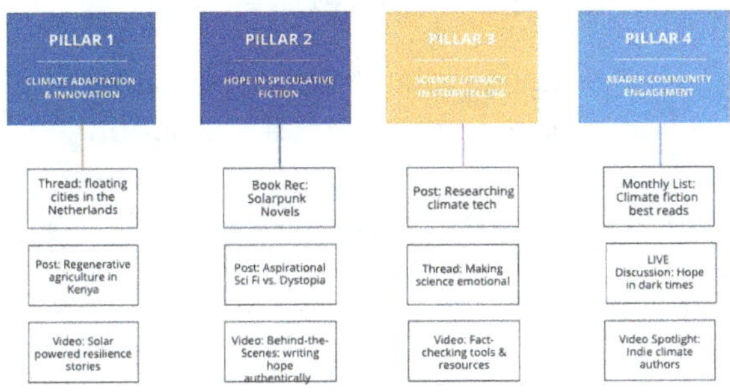

Notice how each pillar connects to both your brand and your readers' needs. Pillar 1 serves readers interested in solutions. Pillar 2 reinforces your "hope through ingenuity" positioning. Pillar 3 speaks to your craft. Pillar 4 builds community and positions you within a reader ecosystem.

Example: Memoir Author (Career Transitions)

You write memoir about leaving corporate life to pursue creative work. Your ME Factor is "practical wisdom for career reinvention," and your emotional promise is "validation plus actionable courage." Your reader personas include corporate professionals feeling stuck, mid-career changers, and people seeking permission to choose differently.

Your content pillars might be:

1. **The Psychology of Career Change:** Why transitions feel so hard and what helps
2. **Practical Exit Strategy:** Real tactics for planning career shifts
3. **Creative Life Design:** What life looks like on the other side
4. **Stories of Reinvention:** Interviews and reader stories

Each pillar serves both your positioning and your readers' journey from considering change to taking action.

Step 3: Test Your Pillars Against Your Reader Personas

Go back to your 2-3 reader personas from Chapter 5. For each pillar, ask:

- Would Persona [Name] find this valuable?
- Does this help them on their journey?
- Does this reinforce why my work matters to them?

If a pillar doesn't serve at least one of your personas, either revise it or replace it. Your content pillars exist to build familiarity, trust, and curiosity with your specific readers—not everyone online.

Step 4: Map Content Types to Each Pillar

Each pillar can generate multiple content types. You're not inventing new content for each platform—you're creating once and adapting strategically.

Content types within each pillar might include:

- **Educational posts:** Tips, insights, or explanations related to your pillar theme
- **Personal stories:** Your own experiences that connect to the pillar
- **Reader engagement:** Questions, polls, or conversations that invite participation
- **Curated recommendations:** Books, articles, or resources aligned with the pillar
- **Behind-the-scenes:** Your process, research, or creative journey
- **Book announcements:** New releases, pre-orders, or launch updates framed within your pillar context

The key is that even promotional content—like book announcements—should connect to at least one of your pillars. Your new release isn't just "buy my book." It's positioned within the themes your readers already associate with you. Some authors create anchored content themes tied to specific days—like "Magic Mondays" where a young adult fantasy author shares tidbits and excerpts from her teen witch series. Her target readers come to expect and look forward to this weekly content. That kind of consistent, memorable approach makes visibility realistic rather than exhausting.

For example, under the "Climate Adaptation & Innovation" pillar, our science fiction author might create:

- Short posts about real-world adaptation projects
- Longer essays about how these innovations inform their fiction
- Video content touring innovative spaces (if relevant to

persona platforms)

- Newsletter deep-dives linking current events to story themes
- Book launch content framed as "this is the hopeful future I imagined based on real innovation"

A note on visual content: Every content type you create for social platforms requires an accompanying graphic. Your visual is how you engineer a readers' first impression—it **instantly** shapes how they'll feel and what they'll think about your content before they read a single word. In milliseconds, your graphic determines whether readers stop scrolling and engage with your text at all. The graphic isn't decoration; it's the gatekeeper to your message. Chapter 9 provides practical guidance on creating graphics efficiently using free tools like Canva, AI image generators, or royalty-free photo sites.

The pillar stays consistent. The format and specific content type adapt to platform, audience, and purpose.

CALIBRATION: Are Your Content Pillars Working?

Content pillars aren't set-it-and-forget-it. They should evolve as you learn what resonates with your readers and what sustains your energy. Here's how to know if your system is working—or needs adjustment.

Warning Signs Your Pillars Need Revision:

✖ **You're avoiding content creation entirely:** If your pillars feel like homework, they're not aligned with your authentic interests. Revise until you're working with themes you genuinely enjoy exploring.

✗ **Your content feels repetitive within weeks:** Your pillars might be too narrow. Can you expand the scope without losing strategic focus?

✗ **Readers aren't engaging, even with consistent posting:** Your pillars might serve your interests but not your readers' needs. Revisit your personas—what are you missing?

✗ **You're struggling to generate ideas within your pillars:** Either your pillars are too rigid, or you've defined them at the wrong altitude. Try zooming in (more specific) or zooming out (broader theme).

✗ **Your pillars feel disconnected from your books:** Go back to your ME Factor and emotional promise. Your pillars should reinforce your brand, not run parallel to it.

Indicators of Success:

✔ **Content creation feels easier, not harder:** You sit down knowing what you're creating content about, even if you're deciding on the specific angle in the moment.

✔ **Readers start associating you with your themes:** People tag you in related content, ask your perspective on topics within your pillars, or mention your themes when describing your work.

✔ **You can generate multiple content ideas quickly:** Each pillar gives you enough scope to create varied content without ever feeling stuck.

✔ **Your content feels aligned with your author brand:** When you post, it reinforces (rather than dilutes) the brand through-line you defined in Chapter 7.

✔ **You're building familiarity with your specific reader personas:** The people engaging with your content match the personas you defined. They're not just random followers—they're your readers.

If you're not sure whether your pillars are working yet, that's completely normal. Smart content strategy is iterative and you won't know what resonates until you test it. Give your pillars at least 6-8 weeks of consistent use before evaluating for possible revision. Cultivating strategic clarity is a gradual process.

Chapter 13 will walk you through metrics that matter (not vanity metrics), and Chapter 18 will give you a quarterly review process for evaluating what's working. For now, focus on defining pillars that feel authentic and strategic. You've got this.

WORKROOM: Content Pillar Development

LEVEL 1: ESSENTIAL (Start Here) – 30 minutes

Grab your ME Factor, emotional promise, reader personas, and brand through-line from previous chapters.

Step 1 (10 minutes): Read through your strategic work and make note of every theme that appears more than once. Don't overthink it—just capture what you notice.

Step 2 (10 minutes): Circle the 3-5 themes that feel most authentic to you AND most valuable to your target reader personas. These are your content pillar candidates.

Step 3 (10 minutes): For each pillar, write one sentence describing why it matters to your readers and one sentence describing why you care about it. If you struggle with either sentence, that pillar might not be the right fit.

That's it. You now have draft content pillars. You don't need to create content yet—you're building the strategic framework first.

LEVEL 2: IF YOU WANT TO GO DEEPER (Optional)

Once you have your 3-5 pillar candidates, take another hour to test and refine them.

Persona Check (20 minutes): For each pillar, note which of your 2-3 reader personas would care about this theme and why. If a pillar doesn't serve at least one persona, revise or replace it.

Content Brainstorm (20 minutes): Under each pillar, brainstorm a few specific content ideas. Can you easily generate them? If you're stuck, the pillar might be too narrow or too broad.

Platform Map (20 minutes): Looking at where your personas spend time (from Chapter 5) and note which platforms each pillar might work best on. You're not committing to anything yet—you're just noticing where content might naturally fit.

LEVEL 3: DEEP DIVE (Come back to this over time)

This is the comprehensive version you can return to over weeks or months as you refine your content strategy.

Content Audit (Ongoing): If you've been creating content already, review your last 3-6 months of posts. What themes emerged naturally? Which got the most meaningful engagement (not just likes—actual connection with readers)? Do those themes align with your pillar candidates, or do you need to revise?

Competitive Intelligence (1-2 hours): Look at 3-4 authors with similar positioning. What are their content themes? Notice what's already saturated vs. where there might be white space for your unique perspective.

Content Calendar Framework (Ongoing): This isn't about scheduling every post for the next three months. Instead, create a simple rotation: if you have four content pillars, you might post Pillar 1 on Mondays, Pillar 2 every other Wednesday, Pillar 3 on first Fridays, and Pillar 4 as bonus content. Or you might batch-create all Pillar 1 content for a month, then move to Pillar 2. Find a rhythm that feels realistic for you.

Refinement Cycle (Quarterly): Every 90 days, review which pillars are serving your brand, and which might need adjustment. Content strategy isn't set in stone—it evolves as you continue learning what resonates with your actual readers.

You've just defined the strategic themes that organize all your content. This isn't busywork—it's the framework that makes visibility possible. In Chapter 9, we'll look at how to express your brand consistently across different platforms without compromising your message. But for now, you have something few authors develop: strategic clarity about what you're creating content around and why.

That clarity changes everything.

CHAPTER 9

BRAND EXPRESSION: SHOWING UP CONSISTENTLY

Your author brand isn't a logo—it's a promise that travels.

When a reader encounters you on Instagram, then finds your website, then subscribes to your newsletter, they should experience the same *essential you* across all three touchpoints. Not necessarily identical content—but a consistent through-line that makes you recognizable and memorable. That consistency is what transforms scattered visibility into strategic brand building.

Most authors approach platforms as separate projects: one voice for social media, another for their website, something different for email. The result? Readers can't connect the dots between touchpoints, and every impression starts from zero instead of building on the last. But when your brand expression is consistent while adapting to platform strengths, readers recognize you everywhere they encounter you. That recognition becomes trust. And trust becomes readership.

You've defined your content pillars in Chapter 8—the themes that organize what you talk about. This chapter addresses how you express those themes across different platforms in ways that feel native to each space while maintaining your brand integrity.

WHAT: Brand Consistency vs. Platform Adaptation

Brand consistency doesn't mean posting identical content everywhere. It means maintaining a recognizable through-line in how you show up, regardless of platform. Your target readers should be able to identify your content in their feed before they even see your name.

Your Author Brand vs. Individual Book Brands

Before we go further, let's clarify something critical: Your author brand is universal across everything you write—it's not tied to individual books or specific genres. Individual books may have different covers, titles, plots, or topics, but your author brand remains constant.

Your author brand through-line isn't your genre or even your content pillars—it's **how your books make readers feel.**

Think of it like a film director's signature style. You can recognize a Wes Anderson film (The Royal Tenenbaums—

quirky, offbeat) or a Nora Ephron rom-com (When Harry Met Sally—warm, optimistic) regardless of the specific story.

This matters because your content pillars, visual brand, verbal brand, and platform presence should reinforce YOUR consistent brand—not shift with every book release. Readers follow authors, not just books. They're investing in the experience you consistently deliver, whatever the specific story or topic.

The Elements of Brand Consistency

That through-line includes:

- **Verbal brand elements:** Your tone, vocabulary, the way you frame ideas
- **Visual brand elements:** Color palette, typography choices, image style
- **Thematic consistency:** Your content pillars expressed in platform-appropriate ways
- **Emotional consistency:** The feeling readers associate with your work (your emotional promise from Chapter 3)

Platform adaptation means respecting the native language and technical requirements of each space. What works on LinkedIn won't work on TikTok. A Twitter thread isn't a blog post. Instagram Reels demand different pacing than YouTube videos. The strategic balance: Your brand stays consistent. Your execution adapts.

WHY: Consistent Brand Expression Multiplies Impact

The Data: Market research on integrated brand communication demonstrates that consistent messaging across multiple touchpoints increases brand recognition by up to 80% compared to inconsistent messaging. But here's what matters for authors: consistency doesn't just make you more recognizable—it makes you more trustworthy.

When readers encounter you on social media, then visit your website, then receive your newsletter, they're unconsciously assessing whether you're the same person in all three places. Inconsistency raises questions: Which version is real? Can I trust what I'm seeing? But when your brand expression remains consistent, readers relax into familiarity. They recognize you. They remember you. They trust you enough to try your books.

For the romance author who writes second-chance love stories:

Imagine a reader discovers you through a TikTok video where you talk about emotional vulnerability in fiction. Your visual style is honest, warm and approachable. They like what they see, so they visit your website. There, they find the same style, the same honest tone in your bio, the same focus on emotional authenticity. Curious, they subscribe to your newsletter. Your welcome email arrives with that same warmth and vulnerability. By the time they see your book, they already know what you stand for. The decision to buy feels natural, not risky.

Now imagine instead that your TikTok profile is warm and vulnerable, your website is corporate and formal, and your newsletter is chatty and humorous. Same reader, but now they're confused. Who are you, really? The disconnect creates friction. They might still buy your book, but you've lost the positive effects of consistent brand impressions.

This is why brand consistency matters: it eliminates the friction between discovery and trust. Every consistent engagement reinforces the last, building recognition that leads to readership.

Consistent brand expression also solves three practical challenges:

1. Platform Fatigue: When you're inventing a new version of yourself for every platform, content creation becomes exhausting. But when you're expressing the same essential brand in platform-appropriate ways, the work becomes worthwhile.

2. Audience Confusion: Readers who follow you in multiple places shouldn't feel like they're following different people. Consistency helps them recognize you instantly, regardless of where they encounter your content.

3. Strategic Dilution: When your brand expression varies wildly across platforms, you're not building one strong brand— you're building several weak ones. Consistency concentrates your impact instead of scattering it.

Some authors create anchored content themes tied to specific days—like "Magic Mondays" where a young adult fantasy author shares tidbits and excerpts from her teen witch series. Her target readers come to expect and look forward to this weekly content as a result of her consistent, memorable approach.

The authors who build recognizable brands aren't present on more platforms—they're more consistent across the platforms where their target readers spend time.

HOW: Building Your Cross-Platform Brand System

Building consistent brand expression across platforms isn't about rigid uniformity—it's about defining the elements that remain constant while giving yourself flexibility to adapt.

Define Your Verbal Brand Elements

Start with the voice and language patterns that feel authentically you and align with your emotional promise. These should remain consistent everywhere you show up.

Consider:

- **Tone:** Are you conversational or polished? Warm or authoritative? Humorous or serious? Choose 2-3 adjectives that describe your consistent tone.
- **Vocabulary:** What words or phrases do you use repeatedly? What language feels natural to you? What terms resonate with your target readers?
- **Sentence structure:** Do you write in long, flowing sentences or short, punchy ones? Do you ask lots of questions or make declarative statements?
- **Topics you consistently address:** Your content pillars from Chapter 8

For instance, a historical fiction author whose emotional promise centers on "immersive escape with emotional depth" might define their verbal brand as: warm and literary, uses sensory language, asks reflective questions, balances historical detail with emotional resonance.

Identify 3-5 verbal brand elements that feel true to you and align with what your target readers respond to. These elements should appear in everything you write, regardless of platform.

Define Your Visual Brand Elements

Even if you're not a designer, you can create effective graphics that make your content recognizable and strategic.

Graphics as Strategic Communication Tools

In Chapter 8, you learned that graphics aren't optional—they're the gatekeeper to your message. Now let's go deeper: your graphics don't just maintain brand consistency. They tell stories, create emotional impact, and communicate your positioning before readers process a single word.

The strategic power of visuals: The human brain can process images in as little as 13 milliseconds. On mobile social media, users spend an average of 1.7 seconds deciding whether to engage with content or scroll past. Your graphic does that work instantly—creating an emotional impression that determines whether readers stop or keep moving.

This means your visual strategy serves two purposes: **First, consistency**—your graphics maintain recognizable visual identity across platforms (color palette, typography, style) so readers know it's you immediately. **Second, communication**—your graphics express your content pillars visually, reinforcing your message and emotional promise through imagery, design choices, theme, vibe, and composition.

Creating graphics efficiently: You don't need to be a designer to create effective graphics. You need strategic clarity about what you're communicating and access to the right tools.

Free and low-cost tools:

Canva (free and pro versions) offers social media templates pre-sized for every platform. Choose templates aligned with your visual brand elements, customize with your colors and fonts, and save as templates you can reuse. Canva's brand kit feature (pro version) stores your exact color codes and fonts for one-click consistency.

AI image generators (Midjourney, DALL-E, Stable Diffusion, Leonardo.ai) create custom images based on text prompts. Useful for creating unique, on-brand visuals that don't exist in stock photo libraries. Quality varies—expect multiple versions before getting usable results.

Royalty-free photo sites (Unsplash, Pexels, Pixabay) offer high-resolution photos free for commercial use. Search for images that evoke the emotional tone of your content pillars. A memoir author writing about resilience might use images of light breaking through clouds; a business author writing about innovation might use images of team collaboration or forward momentum.

Critical technical requirement: Every graphic must be high resolution for the platform you're posting to. Low-resolution images look unprofessional and undermine your credibility regardless of how good your design is. Use platform-specific dimensions (listed later in this chapter) and export at 72 dpi minimum for web, higher for print materials.

Aligning graphics with your content pillars: Each of your 3-5 content pillars should have a recognizable visual approach that readers associate with that theme.

Example: The climate fiction author from Chapter 8 might use:

- Climate Adaptation pillar: Real-world photos of innovative infrastructure, bright hopeful tones
- Hope in Speculative Fiction pillar: Illustrated future cityscapes, optimistic color palette
- Science Literacy pillar: Diagrams, infographics, educational visual style
- Reader Community pillar: Photos of books, readers, book aesthetic

Readers begin associating visual styles with types of content from you—creating pattern recognition that builds familiarity.

Create once, adapt everywhere: Don't create entirely new graphics for each platform. Create one strong visual, then adapt it to platform specifications: Instagram post (square) uses the full graphic; Instagram Story (vertical) reformats to vertical dimensions; Twitter/X (horizontal) crops to landscape; newsletter header uses the same visual elements in email-optimized dimensions. Same message, same brand, adapted to technical requirements. This is how you maintain visual consistency without spending hours designing for every platform.

Your graphics aren't decoration. They're strategic tools that have the power to *engineer* a viewer's first impression, communicate your positioning, and determine whether your brilliant content ever gets read. Invest the time to create a simple, repeatable visual system—it's one of the highest-leverage activities in your platform strategy.

Book Trailers: From Visible to Memorable in 30 Seconds

People are busy, sometimes even too busy to read a book

synopsis. A 30-40 second book trailer lets a potential reader sit back and be entertained, transported, pulled into the immersive world of your story or business premise through the potent combination of text + video clips + music. Book trailers are your emotional promise-in-action, showing your readers how your book will make them feel and giving them a taste of that emotional experience in less than a minute. A well-crafted book synopsis can make your book visible, but a book trailer makes it memorable.

Tools: Lumen5 for landscape-oriented trailers that can be easily viewed on Twitter/X, Facebook, or LinkedIn. Or use Canva's portrait-oriented video templates for creating book trailers to share on Instagram Reels or TikTok.

Maintaining Brand Consistency Across Different Genres or Topics

If you write across different genres or topics, you might be wondering: How do I maintain brand consistency when my books look so different on the surface?

How your books make readers feel remains constant even when the packaging changes.

A nonfiction author who writes both self-help and business books might seem to be writing for different audiences. But if the emotional through-line is "empowered clarity to create positive change," both types of books deliver that same feeling. One helps individuals understand why they've been stuck and find a path forward. The other helps organizations understand resistance and navigate change. Different packaging, same emotional experience.

A fiction author who writes both true crime thrillers and cozy mysteries has completely different genre conventions and covers. But if the emotional through-line is "justice served with compassion for human complexity," both deliver that promise. Different tone and violence level, but the same reassurance that justice prevails while honoring why people do what they do.

Your target readers aren't defined by genre—they're seeking the specific emotional experience you consistently deliver. Your platform presence, content pillars, and visual brand should communicate that emotional promise, not the specifics of your current book's genre or topic.

Understand Platform-Specific Requirements

Each platform has technical specifications and cultural norms that affect how you express your brand. Ignoring these requirements means your content won't display properly or won't feel native to the platform.

Image Orientation and Dimensions:

- Instagram Feed Posts: Vertical (1080 x 1440 pixels, 3:4 ratio—recommended for 2026) or portrait (1080 x 1350 pixels, 4:5 ratio); square (1080 x 1080 pixels) takes up less feed space
- Instagram Stories & Reels: Vertical (1080 x 1920 pixels, 9:16 ratio)
- Facebook Posts: Landscape or square (1200 x 630 pixels for link previews)
- Twitter/X: Landscape (1200 x 675 pixels, 16:9 ratio)
- TikTok: Vertical video (1080 x 1920 pixels, 9:16 ratio)
- LinkedIn: Landscape for posts (1200 x 630 pixels)
- Pinterest: Vertical (1000 x 1500 pixels, 2:3 ratio)
- YouTube: Horizontal video (1920 x 1080 pixels, 16:9 ratio)

Platform Cultural Norms:

- **Instagram:** Visual-first, story-driven, personal or aspirational
- **Twitter/X:** Text-first, conversational, quick observations or threads
- **TikTok:** Video-native, entertainment-forward, fast-paced
- **LinkedIn:** Professional context, longer-form thought leadership
- **Facebook:** Community-building, longer captions work, group-focused
- **Newsletter/Email:** Longer-form, more intimate, subscriber-only insights

Your visual brand elements need to work within these specifications. You're not changing your color palette for each platform—you're formatting your consistent brand to meet technical requirements.

Create Platform-Specific Adaptation Guidelines

For each platform where your target readers spend time (identified in Chapter 5), define how your brand adapts while staying recognizable.

Example: Science Fiction Author (Climate Fiction)

Instagram (Primary platform - visual learners interested in climate solutions):

- Visual style: Real-world climate innovation photos with warm, hopeful color overlays
- Tone: Conversational and curious, asking questions in captions

- Content mix: 60% climate adaptation examples, 20% behind-the-scenes writing, 20% book recommendations
- Format: Carousel posts for multi-image storytelling, Reels for short video tours

Newsletter (Deepest engagement with all personas):

- Visual style: Same color palette in header design, minimal graphics
- Tone: Slightly more reflective than Instagram, more room for nuance
- Content mix: Deep dives on any pillar, serialized content, exclusive updates
- Format: 300-600 word essays, one main piece per newsletter

Twitter/X (Secondary platform - science enthusiasts):

- Visual style: Landscape images of innovations, quote graphics from research
- Tone: Same conversational curiosity, more concise
- Content mix: Quick observations, threads connecting news to story themes
- Format: Short posts with links, occasional threads

Notice how the brand stays consistent (tone, color palette, content pillars) while the execution adapts to platform strengths and technical requirements.

Website as Your Brand Anchor

Your website is the one platform you fully control. It should represent the most complete, polished version of your brand and serve as the reference point for all other platforms.

Essential website brand elements:

- **Homepage:** Immediately communicates your ME Factor and emotional promise
- **About page:** Your bio in your authentic voice, explaining what readers can count on from you
- **Books page:** Consistent book cover presentation, descriptions that reinforce your brand
- **Contact/Newsletter signup:** Easy ways for interested readers to stay connected
- **Visual consistency:** Your defined color palette, typography, and image style throughout

Discoverability matters: Use the reader language you captured in Chapter 4 naturally throughout your website - in page titles, headers, and book descriptions. When readers Google phrases like "dark literary thriller morally gray" or "leadership books for nonprofits," your site appears because you're using their search language. This is basic SEO, and it's essential for being found.

Your website shouldn't feel like a different person created it than the person showing up on social media. The sophistication level can be higher—websites allow for more polish—but the essential brand should be unmistakable.

Use Your Newsletter as Brand Deepening

Email is the most intimate platform—readers have invited you into their inbox. Your newsletter should feel like the most authentic, developed version of your brand voice.

Newsletter brand consistency:

- **Welcome sequence:** New subscribers immediately

understand who you are and what to expect

- **Regular cadence:** Consistency in timing builds trust and anticipation
- **Voice consistency:** Same tone as other platforms, slightly more conversational or in-depth
- **Visual elements:** Header design, color palette, typography consistent with other brand touchpoints
- **Content pillars:** Newsletter content should align with your defined pillars, often going deeper than social posts

The goal isn't to repurpose social content into newsletters—it's to offer newsletter-exclusive depth while maintaining the same essential brand that readers recognize from other touchpoints.

CALIBRATION: Is Your Brand Expression Consistent?

Your brand expression should feel coherent across platforms without feeling cookie-cutter. Here's how to know if you're achieving that balance—or if adjustments are needed.

Warning Signs Your Brand Expression Needs Work:

✖ **You feel like a different person on each platform:** If you're performing a character rather than being a consistent version of yourself, readers will sense the artificiality.

✖ **Readers don't recognize you across platforms:** If someone follows you on Instagram but doesn't realize they're already subscribed to your newsletter, your brand isn't consistent enough.

✖ **You're getting follower growth but no book sales:**

Visibility without brand coherence means readers don't connect your content to your books.

✖ Your content doesn't display properly on platforms: If images are getting cropped awkwardly or text is unreadable, you're not adapting to technical requirements.

✖ Creating content for each platform feels like starting from scratch: If there's no through-line connecting your work across platforms, you're missing the efficiency of brand consistency.

Indicators of Success:

✔ Readers mention finding you in multiple places: "I saw you on Instagram, then found your newsletter, and now I'm reading your book" is the dream trajectory.

✔ Your content feels immediately recognizable: Even without seeing your name, your target readers can identify your posts by style, tone, or visual approach.

✔ Platform adaptation feels natural, not forced: You're not trying to be someone you're not—you're expressing yourself appropriately for each space.

✔ Content creation feels more efficient: You're not reinventing your brand for each platform—you're adapting one consistent brand across spaces.

✔ New followers convert to email subscribers and book readers: Brand consistency creates a clear path from discovery to deeper engagement.

If you're finding that your brand feels inconsistent, start with your verbal brand elements. Voice is easier to control than visual design, and it has just as much impact on recognition. Make sure your tone, vocabulary, and content pillars remain consistent, then work on visual alignment.

WORKROOM: Cross-Platform Brand Development

LEVEL 1: ESSENTIAL (Start Here) – 30 minutes

Step 1 (10 minutes): Write down 3 adjectives that describe your authentic voice and tone. Test them: Do these feel true to you? Would your target readers respond to this tone?

Step 2 (10 minutes): Choose 3-5 colors that feel aligned with your emotional promise and genre expectations. You can use a tool like Coolors.co to explore palettes or simply identify colors you're naturally drawn to.

Step 3 (10 minutes): Review your current online presence (website, social media, newsletter if you have them). Circle one element of verbal or visual inconsistency you want to fix first. Just one. You're building consistency, not perfection.

LEVEL 2: IF YOU WANT TO GO DEEPER (Optional)

Once you have your core brand elements defined, spend an hour creating basic adaptation guidelines.

Platform Audit (20 minutes): List the platforms where your target readers spend time (from Chapter 5). For each platform, note the technical requirements (image dimensions, video orientation) and cultural norms (formal vs. casual, text vs.

visual, short vs. long).

Adaptation Guidelines (25 minutes): For your top 2-3 platforms, write 2-3 sentences describing how your brand adapts to that space while staying consistent. What stays the same? What changes?

Visual Brand Kit (15 minutes): Using Canva or another simple design tool, create 2-3 templates with your color palette and typography. These become your go-to formats for quick content creation.

LEVEL 3: DEEP DIVE (Come back to this over time)

This is the comprehensive version you can return to as you refine your cross-platform brand.

Website SEO Basics (After Launch): Review your website and naturally add 5-7 of your strongest keyword phrases from Chapter 4 into your homepage, about page, and book descriptions. Read everything aloud - if it sounds forced, rewrite it naturally. Keywords should enhance clarity, not clutter it.

Brand Guidelines Document (2-3 hours): Create a simple reference document with your verbal brand elements, color palette, fonts, image style preferences, and platform-specific adaptation notes.

Cross-Platform Content Flow (Ongoing): Plan how content flows across platforms. For example: Monday Instagram post becomes Wednesday newsletter topic becomes Friday Twitter thread. You're adapting one idea across multiple touchpoints.

Quarterly Brand Audit (Every 90 days): Review your last

three months of content across all platforms. Does it feel cohesive? Where do you see inconsistency? What's working well that you want to do more of?

You've just defined how your brand travels across platforms without losing itself in translation – well done! This isn't about being everywhere—it's about being recognizably you wherever your target readers encounter you. In Chapter 10, we'll shift from brand expression to strategic assessment, applying business diagnostic tools to your author career. But for now, you have something powerful: a system for showing up consistently without sacrificing platform-appropriate adaptation.

That system becomes the foundation for successful market visibility.

PART IV

DIAGNOSTICS: WHAT'S WORKING (AND WHAT'S NOT)

This is where "Self" meets the "Market" through objective diagnostics. With identity, market knowledge, and brand clarity established, you can now assess your position strategically.

In this section, debut authors will find professional assessment tools to evaluate opportunities, platforms, and strategies before investing time and money—so you build strategically from the start.

Published authors will discover what's working in your current approach and where adjustments could create breakthrough results. Your SWOT analysis will reveal which efforts to double down on, which to abandon, and where your biggest leverage points are.

Returning authors will get an honest audit of your current position—your strengths in today's market, what's no longer serving you, and where the real opportunities are now.

CHAPTER 10

SWOT - YOUR SECRET EDGE

Your writing career is not just a creative pursuit—it's a strategic asset that deserves the same analytical rigor you'd apply to any other professional endeavor.

What if you could step back and see your entire author career with the perspective of a seasoned strategist? What becomes possible when you have a framework for honest, actionable assessment of where you are and where you're headed?

That's exactly what a professional SWOT analysis gives you.

WHAT: SWOT as Strategic Self-Assessment

SWOT stands for Strengths, Weaknesses, Opportunities, and

Threats. It's a classic business strategy tool that helps organizations understand their competitive position and make informed decisions about where to invest resources.

For authors, a SWOT analysis is a structured framework for honest self-assessment. It's the moment you step back from the day-to-day work of writing and marketing to ask: Where am I truly strong? Where am I genuinely struggling? What opportunities exist that I'm positioned to capture? And what external forces might create challenges if I don't get ahead of them?

This isn't overthinking. It's disciplined insight.

Strengths are the assets you already possess—your unique skills, established platforms, professional networks, genre expertise, and audience relationships that give you competitive advantages.

Weaknesses are the gaps in your capabilities or resources—the skills you haven't developed, tools you haven't yet mastered, platforms you're not leveraging, or the systems you lack that create friction in your progress.

Opportunities are external conditions you can leverage— emerging market trends, underserved reader niches, untapped platforms, or professional connections that could accelerate your visibility.

Threats are external forces beyond your control—algorithm changes, market saturation, economic shifts, or competitive pressures that could create challenges if you don't plan for them.

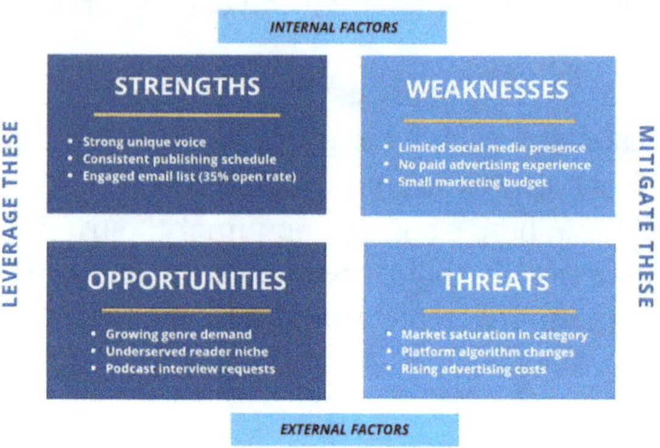

Here's what makes SWOT powerful for authors: Instead of being immersed in the daily work of writing, editing, and promoting, you step back to see everything objectively. This shift helps you separate what you control (strengths and weaknesses) from what you don't (opportunities and threats), so you can think clearly—without judgment—about where you are now, what the future could look like, and how best to get there. That clarity shows you where to invest your limited energy, creativity, and budget, lifting you above your competition and giving you a significant edge.

WHY: Strategic Assessment Changes Everything

Authors who regularly conduct strategic self-assessments adapt quickly, capitalize on opportunities, and build fulfilling careers.

The Data: Research on business strategy shows that organizations that conduct regular competitive assessments are 33% more likely to outperform their competitors. The same principle applies to writing careers. When you understand your true position, you can make decisions that move you forward rather than exhaust you with misaligned effort.

Think about when you might benefit from a quick SWOT snapshot:

You're launching a new series and unsure how to position it. You're considering a major shift—new genre, different pen name, or trying a new platform. Your sales have plateaued and you're not sure why. You're overwhelmed by marketing advice and can't figure out what to prioritize first. You're about to make a significant investment—hiring a publicist, running ads, attending a conference—and want to evaluate if it's the right move.

A SWOT gives you a framework for answering these questions pragmatically rather than emotionally.

Consider a debut fantasy author with a background in education and a strong presence on BookTok. His quick SWOT might reveal:

- **Strengths**: Natural on video, understands how to create engaging short-form content
- **Weaknesses**: No email list, never built a newsletter strategy
- **Opportunities**: Fantasy readers on TikTok are hungry for character-driven stories, and the algorithm currently favors book content
- **Threats**: TikTok's algorithm is unpredictable—relying solely on one platform puts his entire visibility strategy at risk

This assessment tells him exactly what to do: leverage his

TikTok strength while simultaneously addressing the newsletter gap. He doesn't need to master every platform or chase every trend. He needs strategic focus.

Now consider a mid-career business author who's published five books through a small press. Her SWOT looks different:

- **Strengths**: Deep industry expertise, loyal client base, niche credibility
- **Weaknesses**: Books have outdated covers and weak Amazon optimization. Social media presence is inconsistent.
- **Opportunities**: Her corporate clients regularly ask for book recommendations, but she's never created a systematic way to convert that interest into bulk sales
- **Threats**: Younger consultants with strong personal brands are increasingly visible in her space

Her strategy is clear: invest in a visual brand refresh, optimize Amazon presence, and build a more consistent social media presence. She doesn't need to become an influencer—she needs to leverage her professional credibility to build more visibility and engagement where it matters.

The difference between these two authors isn't talent or work ethic. It's strategic perspective about where they are and what they need to do next.

Without this kind of assessment, authors waste time on strategies that don't serve them. They see another author succeeding on Instagram and assume they should be there too —without considering whether their readers are even on that platform. They invest in expensive book trailers without first addressing the weak positioning that could be limiting discoverability.

A SWOT analysis keeps you from chasing trends and helps you invest your limited time and energy where it counts.

HOW: Conducting Your SWOT

The most effective SWOT analysis is both quick and actionable. You're not creating a 50-page strategic plan—you're gaining perspective.

Identifying Your Strengths

Start with what's genuinely working. Your strengths are the assets that differentiate you or give you advantages other authors don't have.

Ask yourself:

- What professional experience or expertise do I have that informs my work or gives me credibility?
- What platforms or channels have I already built where I have engaged audiences?
- What specific skills make certain marketing activities easier for me? (Natural networker? Confident speaker? Skilled visual designer? Compelling storyteller in short form?)
- What relationships or networks could amplify my work?
- What aspects of my author brand are already clear and consistent?

Be specific. "I'm good at social media" isn't a strength. "I have 3,000 engaged followers on LinkedIn who regularly comment on my posts about leadership" is a strength. "I'm a strong writer" isn't strategically useful. "I can translate complex psychological concepts into accessible, story-driven explanations" is a strength you can leverage.

Acknowledging Your Weaknesses

This is where honesty matters most. Your weaknesses aren't character flaws—they're gaps in your current capabilities or resources.

Ask yourself:

- What marketing activities consistently feel overwhelming or get deprioritized?
- What platforms have I neglected or never built?
- What skills do I lack that limit my ability to execute effectively?
- What systems or processes do I lack that could add efficiency?
- Is my author brand unclear or inconsistent?

Be honest, but don't spiral. "I'm terrible at social media" isn't useful. "I've never developed a consistent posting strategy, and I don't understand how to create content that drives book sales" is actionable. That's a weakness you can address.

Recognizing Your Opportunities

Opportunities are external conditions you can leverage—things happening in your market, your genre, or the broader publishing landscape that you're positioned to capture.

Ask yourself:

- What trends are emerging in my genre or niche that

align with my work?

- What reader communities or platforms are growing where my target readers congregate?
- What gaps exist in my market that my work could fill? (Revisit Chapter 6 if needed.)
- What professional connections or partnerships could amplify my visibility?
- What upcoming cultural moments, events, or conversations does my work connect to?

For a science fiction author writing climate fiction, the opportunity might be growing mainstream interest in environmental themes and the rise of climate fiction as a recognized subgenre. For a productivity author, the opportunity might be the post-pandemic shift toward remote work and corresponding demand for time management strategies.

Opportunities are time sensitive. Look at what's emerging and position yourself strategically before the window closes.

Anticipating Your Threats

Threats are external forces that could create challenges—things you can't control but need to plan for.

Ask yourself:

- What changes in algorithms, platforms, or distribution channels could affect my visibility?
- What competitive pressures exist? (More authors entering my niche? Established authors in my space releasing new books?)
- What economic or cultural shifts could reduce demand for my type of work?
- What dependencies do I have that create risk? (Relying

entirely on one platform? One distribution channel? One marketing strategy?)

For an author whose entire platform is built on Twitter/X, the threat is obvious: platform instability, ownership changes, and algorithm shifts could eliminate visibility overnight. For an author writing in an increasingly crowded subgenre, the threat is market saturation and reader fatigue.

Threats are opportunities to diversify, adapt, and build resilience into your strategy.

Pre-Publication SWOT: Planning Your Debut Launch

If you haven't yet published, a SWOT analysis can still apply—you're just assessing different elements.

Strengths (What You Already Have):

- Professional expertise informing your forthcoming book's credibility
- Existing networks (industry contacts, professional communities)
- Transferable skills (public speaking, design, teaching experience)
- Platform foundation (even basic: website, small newsletter, active LinkedIn)
- Unique perspective differentiating your work

Example: A debut memoir author has 20 years' experience as a hospice nurse (insider perspective on end-of-life care), a previous TEDx talk on grief (public speaking experience, small following), and a professional network in healthcare (potential early readers).

Weaknesses (What You're Building):

- No published track record or reviews
- Limited author platform
- Unfamiliarity with publishing processes
- No social proof yet

Opportunities (What You Can Claim):

- Market gaps your research revealed
- Emerging trends you can ride from the start
- Underserved reader segments
- Professional connections willing to support a debut
- Media hooks tied to your background

Threats (What to Plan For):

- Building author credibility from the ground up
- Competing with established authors
- Platform algorithm changes
- Slow initial sales while building awareness

Actions You Can Take Now:

Based on your pre-publication SWOT, take these concrete steps 3-6 months before launch:

To leverage your strengths:

- Reach out to 10-15 people in your professional network who match your reader persona—invite them to join your advance reader team
- Audit which platforms showcase your existing skills best (if you're a strong speaker, prioritize video/podcast; if you're visual, focus on Instagram)

- Document your unique expertise or perspective in a one-paragraph bio you'll use across all platforms

To address your weaknesses:

- Start building your email list NOW (aim for 100+ subscribers before launch)
- Create a simple 3-month pre-launch content calendar using your pillars from Chapter 8
- Set up Amazon Author Central and draft your Amazon metadata (book synopsis, author bio) even before your book goes live

To capture your opportunities:

- Identify 5-7 podcasts, blogs, or media outlets where your unique background creates a story angle
- Research 3-5 bookstores or libraries in your area and prepare your pitch (Chapter 15) before publication
- Join 2-3 online communities where your target readers congregate—start engaging authentically now, not just when you have a book to sell

To mitigate your threats:

- Start building a presence on 2 platforms
- Set realistic first-month sales expectations based on your list size and network reach
- Create a 90-day post-launch plan (Chapter 18) so you're not scrambling after release

Your pre-publication SWOT becomes your launch roadmap. The "Connecting the Dots" framework shows you exactly how to turn this assessment into strategy.

Connecting the Dots

Once you've identified your strengths, weaknesses, opportunities, and threats, the real work begins: turning that assessment into strategic decisions.

Look for where things overlap:

Strength + Opportunity: Where can you leverage your existing assets to capitalize on emerging opportunities? This is your highest-*ROI* focus area.

Strength + Threat: How can you use your strengths to address external challenges? This is your *defensive strategy*.

Weakness + Opportunity: What capabilities do you need to develop to capture opportunities you're currently not positioned for? This is your *skill-building priority*.

Weakness + Threat: What gaps make you most vulnerable to external pressures? This is your *risk mitigation focus*.

Let's return to our fantasy author:

- **Strength (BookTok presence) + Opportunity (fantasy readers on TikTok)**: Double down on video content and engage authentically with fantasy readers.
- **Strength (video skills) + Threat (platform dependence)**: Repurpose TikTok content for YouTube Shorts and Instagram Reels to diversify.
- **Weakness (no email list) + Opportunity (engaged TikTok audience)**: Build a lead magnet and drive TikTok followers to newsletter signup.

- **Weakness (no email list) + Threat (algorithm unpredictability)**: Prioritize building owned channels that aren't subject to platform whims.

His strategy isn't "do everything." It's "leverage BookTok aggressively while simultaneously building platform independence through email."

That's strategic focus.

CALIBRATION: Is Your SWOT Working?

A SWOT analysis is only valuable if it leads to action and adaptation. Here's how to know if your assessment is serving you.

Warning Signs Your SWOT Isn't Working:

✗ **You completed the analysis but didn't change any behaviors or priorities.** A SWOT that doesn't inform decisions is just a list.

✗ **Your SWOT is all strengths and opportunities with no weaknesses or threats.** Every author has gaps and vulnerabilities. If you can't identify yours, dig deeper.

✗ **You identified too many items and now you're overwhelmed.** A useful SWOT is focused. Prioritize only the top 2-3 items in each quadrant.

✗ **Your opportunities and threats aren't actually external.** "I don't post consistently" is a weakness, not a threat. "Algorithm changes" is a threat.

Indicators of Success:

✔ **You have clear priorities.** After completing your SWOT, you know exactly what to focus on next.

✔ **You've made strategic decisions based on your assessment.** Maybe you've stopped trying to build a platform that doesn't serve your readers. Maybe you've invested in learning a skill that addresses a critical weakness.

✔ **You're no longer surprised by setbacks.** Because you identified threats in advance, you have contingency plans.

✔ **You revisit and update your SWOT regularly.** Strategic assessment isn't a one-time event. Authors who treat SWOT as an ongoing practice stay ahead.

✔ **You feel more confident saying no.** A clear SWOT helps you recognize what doesn't serve your strategy.

This book will teach you every skill referenced in your SWOT analysis. If you identified email marketing as a weakness, Chapter 13 will help. If you recognized a need for better platform strategy, Chapter 12 has you covered. If speaking opportunities feel challenging because you don't know how to leverage them, Chapter 17 will guide you.

WORKROOM: SWOT Development

LEVEL 1: ESSENTIAL (Start Here) – 30 minutes

Create a simple four-quadrant grid. Label each quadrant: Strengths, Weaknesses, Opportunities, Threats.

Spend about 7 minutes on each quadrant. Brainstorm freely without editing yourself. Aim for 3-5 items per quadrant.

When the timer goes off, look at your grid and circle the *one* item in each quadrant that feels most significant. Those four circled items are your current strategic focus.

Write one sentence about what you'll do with each of those insights in the next 30 days.

You now have strategic direction.

LEVEL 2: IF YOU WANT TO GO DEEPER

Return to your SWOT grid and ask follow-up questions for each item:

For **Strengths**: How can I leverage this more intentionally? What opportunities does this strength position me to capture?

For **Weaknesses**: What would it take to address this gap? Is this a skill I need to learn, a system I need to build, or a resource I need to acquire?

For **Opportunities**: What would I need to do to capitalize on this? Am I well-positioned to pursue this, or would it require building capabilities I don't currently have?

For **Threats**: How can I reduce this risk? What diversification or contingency planning would make me more resilient?

Now look for connections across quadrants. Where do your strengths and opportunities align? Where do weaknesses and threats intersect? These overlaps tell you where to focus.

LEVEL 3: DEEP DIVE

Schedule quarterly Author SWOT reviews. Set calendar reminders for 90 days from now, six months from now, and one year from now.

Each time, repeat the Level 1 exercise and note what's changed. Your strengths should be increasing; your weaknesses shrinking. New opportunities should be emerging as you build visibility. And threats you identified should feel less threatening because you've planned for them.

You can also conduct a comparative SWOT by analyzing 2-3 authors in your space whose careers you admire. For each author, identify: What strengths do they have that I could develop? What opportunities have they capitalized on that I haven't pursued? What threats have they navigated successfully that I'm currently facing?

This isn't about imitation—it's about pattern recognition. What strategic moves are working in your market? What positioning choices are paying off?

Come back to this over time. Your SWOT isn't static—it evolves as your career does.

This chapter gives you the strategic assessment framework you need before diving into tactical execution. You now know where you stand, what you're working with, and where to focus your energy. That insight is what transforms scattered effort into increased momentum.

Next, we'll apply this same diagnostic rigor to your author platform—because knowing what you have is the first step to knowing what to build.

CHAPTER 11

PLATFORM CHECK: KNOW YOUR POWER

Your author platform isn't a single thing—it's the ecosystem of channels where your brand lives and where readers can find you, learn about your work, and engage.

Platform building is about being strategic about where and how you show up for readers and intentional about your presence on platforms that grow your brand. But this platform is most powerful when all your online channels are aligned.

This chapter will help you assess the channels in your online ecosystem to identify which ones are working for you and deserve your continued attention.

WHAT: Identifying Your Channels

Your author platform is the collection of owned and public channels where your author brand shows up. These are the places where readers can discover you, engage with you, and experience the promise your brand delivers.

Common platform components include:

Owned channels (you control the content):

- Your author website
- Your email newsletter
- Your blog or podcast

Public channels (you control the content but not the platform):

- Social media profiles (Instagram, TikTok, Facebook, LinkedIn, Twitter, etc.)
- Amazon author page
- Goodreads profile
- YouTube channel

Your platform isn't just about using these channels—it's about how they work together to create a consistent, recognizable presence.

The most critical element of an effective author platform is **alignment**. When readers encounter you on one channel and then find you on another, they should know immediately they're in the right place. Same person. Same brand. Same promise.

WHY: Alignment More Than Quantity

It's okay to strive to be visible and recognizable to a broad audience. But your real power as an author is when you become memorable to the target readers who matter most—to your brand, your books, and your legacy.

According to marketing research, it takes 15-20 brand impressions before someone remembers you. When those impressions feel consistent and connected, they grow your reach and visibility exponentially. A reader who sees you on Instagram visits your website, then encounters you on Twitter and experiences the same author each time—and those impressions build recognition and trust.

The Data: Consistent branding across platforms increases brand recognition by up to 80%. When readers consistently encounter your aligned brand, they're more likely to remember you, trust you, and ultimately buy from you. Alignment is the key to becoming memorable to your readers.

Consider a romance author who writes uplifting contemporary love stories with strong female leads. On Instagram, her bio says, "Romance author | HEA guaranteed." Her profile picture is a professional headshot with warm lighting. Her posts are colorful, optimistic, and focus on love, relationships, and emotional connection.

But when a reader clicks through to her website, the site is dark and moody with a stark black-and-white author photo. Her bio says, "Writer of fiction." There's no mention of romance, no warmth, no emotional promise. The reader wonders if they're in the right place. That moment of confusion creates friction.

Now consider a business author who writes about organizational leadership and growth. Her LinkedIn profile says, "Award-winning author of transformational leadership books." Her profile picture is a sharp, professional headshot. Her posts discuss change management, team dynamics, and the human side of business transformation. Her website uses the same headshot, the same positioning statement, and the same visual tone—sleek, sophisticated, grounded. Her newsletter opens with that same positioning statement and reinforces her brand through-line: *practical wisdom that honors both results and people.*

A reader who discovers her on LinkedIn and then visits her website knows immediately: same author, same promise, same brand. Those impressions multiply. Her platform is working.

Alignment amplifies every impression. When your channels work together to reinforce your brand, you're not scattering your impact. You're concentrating it.

HOW: Auditing Your Author Platform

An effective platform audit has three components: assessing alignment, evaluating activity, and setting priorities.

Assessing Alignment Across Channels

Start by documenting every channel where your author brand currently appears. Website, email newsletter, Instagram, TikTok, Facebook, Twitter/X, LinkedIn, Amazon author page, Goodreads—capture them all.

Now audit for alignment across these key elements:

Profile Picture: Use the same (or very similar) professional author photo across all platforms so readers recognize you instantly.

Author Positioning Statement: Your one-sentence description of who you are and what you write—the work you did in Chapter 2 when you defined your ME Factor—should appear consistently everywhere. Your website bio, social media bios, email newsletter header, Amazon author page. Everywhere.

Visual Consistency: Your channels should share a cohesive visual identity. Colors, fonts, and imagery should feel like they belong to the same brand. Your visual brand can adapt to platform requirements while still feeling recognizably yours, like a fantasy author using a magic wand emoji in social media profiles.

Brand Voice: Your tone and language should feel consistent across platforms. Your brand voice (established in Chapter 9) should be recognizable no matter where readers encounter you.

Brand Through-Line: Each channel should reinforce the emotional promise readers can expect from your work. If you write self-improvement books on confidence and empowerment, your online presence should convey that upbeat tone. If you write dark psychological thrillers, your platform presence should reflect that moody atmosphere.

Walk through each channel and note where you have opportunities to strengthen alignment. Where could your profile picture be more consistent? Where is your positioning statement missing? Where could your visual or verbal brand feel more connected?

Evaluating Activity and Engagement

Alignment creates the foundation, and activity shows you where that foundation is generating momentum.

For each channel, gather basic activity data:

Website: Check your analytics. How many visitors per month? Which pages get the most traffic? How long do people stay? Where do they come from? If you don't have analytics installed, add Google Analytics or a similar tool now.

Email Newsletter: What's your open rate? Click-through rate? How many subscribers do you have, and is that list growing? Email platforms like Mailchimp and MailerLite offer comprehensive analytics tools to not only monitor engagement but also to optimize newsletter text and headlines for maximum engagement.

Social Media: For each platform, note your follower count, but more importantly, note the number of likes, comments, shares, or saves your posts receive. Are followers interacting with your content?

Amazon Author Page or Goodreads: How many followers do you have? Do readers engage with your updates?

Again, this is pattern recognition. Where are readers showing up? Where are you getting genuine engagement?

If you have 5,000 followers on Instagram, that's fantastic reach. But if your posts are bringing back minimal likes and comments, some strategic content adjustments can boost engagement significantly. If your newsletter has 800 subscribers with a 45% open rate and readers regularly reply, that's excellent engagement worth building on. Numbers alone don't tell the story—interaction does.

Prioritizing Strategically

If you feel like you're posting on more channels than you can reasonably monitor, scaling back has many strategic advantages. Consider which platforms and activities boost—or drain—your energy. Maybe some of the platforms you're using could be redirected into the 3-4 channels where you get the strongest response. Identify your top channels and pour your energy and creativity into those—and watch them grow.

For each channel, ask yourself:

Is this channel aligned with my brand? If you've been maintaining a platform that doesn't reflect your brand consistently, you have an opportunity to either bring it into alignment or redirect that energy elsewhere.

Is this channel generating meaningful engagement? If you're investing time with only limited interaction, your content strategy could evolve, or your energy could be better utilized on a different platform.

Can I realistically maintain this channel? You might love the idea of a podcast, but if the reality of recording, editing, and promoting episodes feels daunting, it's worth considering whether that format serves your strengths and capacity.

Does this channel reach my target readers? If you write business books for executives and you're spending hours on TikTok where your readers don't congregate, you have an opportunity to reallocate that effort to LinkedIn. Go back to your reader personas from Chapter 5—where do they spend time?

PLATFORM ASSESSMENT MATRIX

Here's what strategic prioritization looks like in practice:

A business author realizes he has a website, a newsletter, Instagram, Facebook, TikTok, and a Goodreads profile. His audit reveals:

- Website: Strong traffic, especially to his blog posts about organizational change
- Newsletter: 1,200 subscribers, 38% open rate, readers regularly reply
- Instagram: 3,000 followers, room to grow engagement
- Facebook: 800 followers, inconsistent posting
- TikTok: 150 followers, sporadic posts
- Goodreads: Solid following, readers engage with his updates

His strategic decision: Focus on website and newsletter (high engagement, aligned with his brand). Maintain Goodreads (low effort and strong reader presence). Pause TikTok and Facebook (energy better spent elsewhere). Experiment with Instagram for three months with a new content strategy—if engagement improves, it becomes a priority platform.

He's not abandoning everything. He's agile and flexible, concentrating effort where it matters most.

A historical fiction author realizes her platform includes:

- Website: Outdated, ready for a refresh
- Newsletter: 400 subscribers, open rates could improve
- LinkedIn: 8,000 followers, strong engagement on posts about historical research
- Twitter: 1,500 followers, moderate engagement
- Speaking engagements: Regular invitations, leads to book sales

Her strategic decision: Refresh website to align with her LinkedIn brand. Revitalize newsletter with better content that serves her LinkedIn audience. Double down on LinkedIn (where her readers are and engagement is high). Maintain Twitter at a lower frequency. Prioritize speaking (direct connection to readers and sales).

Notice neither of these authors is trying to be everywhere. They're being strategic about where their effort is most needed.

CALIBRATION: Is Your Platform Working?

Your platform is working if it's aligned, active, and making you memorable to the readers who matter. You'll recognize the signs.

Warning Signs Your Platform Could Be Stronger:

❌ **Your channels feel disconnected.** Readers who find you on one platform don't immediately recognize you on another. This is an opportunity to strengthen visual and verbal consistency.

❌ **You're maintaining platforms out of obligation rather than strategy.** You keep posting because you think you "should," even though there's little engagement. This energy could be redirected to platforms where your readers congregate.

❌ **You're working from assumptions rather than data.** You're guessing about what's generating results instead of looking at actual engagement metrics.

Indicators of Success:

✔ **Your channels feel cohesive.** A reader who discovers you on Instagram and visits your website knows immediately they're in the right place.

✔ **You're getting meaningful engagement on your priority platforms.** Readers comment, share, reply, and interact.

✔ **You've made strategic decisions about what to maintain and where to focus.** You're concentrating effort on the channels that truly serve your brand and reach your readers.

This book will help you strengthen every component of your platform. If your website needs work, Chapter 12 will guide you on content systems. If your social media needs strategy, Chapter 13 covers that. You don't need to have everything figured out right now.

WORKROOM: Platform Alignment Audit
LEVEL 1: ESSENTIAL (Start Here) – 30 minutes

Create a simple spreadsheet or document with these columns: Channel | Profile Picture | Positioning Statement | Visual Alignment | Brand Voice | Engagement Level

Document every platform where your author brand currently appears: website, newsletter, Instagram, Facebook, LinkedIn, TikTok, Amazon, Goodreads, etc.

For each channel, answer:

- **Profile Picture**: Same as or similar to other channels? Yes/No
- **Positioning Statement**: Present and consistent? Yes/No
- **Visual Alignment**: Feels like the same brand? Yes/No
- **Brand Voice**: Tone matches other channels? Yes/No
- **Engagement Level**: High/Medium/Low (based on actual interaction, not follower count)

Circle the channels with the most "No" answers—those are opportunities for alignment work. Circle the channels with "High" engagement—those deserve continued focus.

Identify one channel to bring into alignment this week and one low-engagement channel to deprioritize or pause.

Done. You now have a clear picture of where your platform has the most potential.

LEVEL 2: IF YOU WANT TO GO DEEPER

For each channel, gather specific activity data:

Website: Install Google Analytics if you haven't already. Note monthly visitors, top pages, average time on site, and traffic sources.

Newsletter: Record subscriber count, average open rate, click-through rate, and whether your list is growing.

Social Media: For each platform, note follower count, average engagement per post (likes, comments, shares, saves), and posting frequency.

Now create a priority matrix. Draw four quadrants:

- **High Alignment + High Engagement**: Your core platforms—maintain and strengthen these
- **High Alignment + Low Engagement**: Opportunity for better content strategy—experiment here
- **Low Alignment + High Engagement**: Bring into alignment immediately—readers are there and will benefit from consistency
- **Low Alignment + Low Engagement**: Consider deprioritizing—your energy might be better leveraged elsewhere

Based on this matrix, write down:

- Which 2-3 channels will be your primary focus for the next 90 days
- Which 1-2 channels you'll bring into alignment
- Which channels you'll use less frequently
- What specific alignment improvements you'll make (update profile picture, add positioning statement, refresh visual design, etc.)

LEVEL 3: DEEP DIVE

Conduct a reader journey audit. Ask 1-2 readers (or friends who fit your target reader profile) to find you online as if they'd just discovered you.

Have them start on one platform (e.g., Instagram) and then visit your website, sign up for your newsletter, and find you on one other social platform. Ask them:

- Did they immediately recognize you across platforms?
- What felt consistent? What felt disconnected?
- Did your brand promise feel clear?
- What could be even stronger?

Their feedback will reveal alignment opportunities you might not see yourself.

Also, schedule quarterly platform audits. Every 90 days, revisit your alignment check and activity data. Note what's changed. Are engagement levels improving on your priority platforms? Have you successfully brought channels into alignment? Are there new platforms that might be worth exploring?

Come back to this regularly. Your platform isn't static—it evolves as your career and reader behaviors change.

This chapter gives you the framework to assess what you have, identify what's working, and focus your effort where it means something. You now have the perspective to know which channels deserve your attention and which ones could benefit from strategic adjustments. And you have the framework to funnel your energy where it creates the most impact.

Next, we'll talk about how to build content systems for those priority platforms—because knowing where to focus is most valuable when you can maintain that presence strategically and sustainably.

PART V

DIGITAL VISIBILITY: FIND YOUR READERS

With your foundation built, you're ready for digital promotion. Your marketing becomes an extension of your brand, not a desperate chase for attention.

In this section, debut authors will learn how to build sustainable visibility without burning out. You'll discover which platforms matter for your readers and how to show up consistently without living on social media.

Published authors will see how to sharpen your digital strategy and replace scattered effort with focused systems that reach the right readers.

Returning authors will catch up on what works now—algorithms have changed, platforms have shifted, and this section shows you how to rebuild visibility strategically.

CHAPTER 12

CONTENT THAT WORKS

If you've ever felt overwhelmed by the pressure to be everywhere, posting constantly, keeping up with every platform and every fleeting trend—you're not alone.

Here's the truth:

You don't need to be on every platform. You don't need to post every day. You don't need to become a social media expert or a content creation machine to build visibility for your work.

What you need is a customized approach that works for you— one that protects your energy, aligns with your brand, and feels manageable.

WHAT: Effective Content Strategy Looks Different Than You Think

Most authors operate under the assumption that effective social media presence requires:

- Being on 5+ platforms
- Posting daily (or multiple times per day)
- Creating endless original content
- Chasing trends and algorithms
- Spending hours every week on content creation

For most authors who are writing, working full-time jobs, managing families and promoting their books, this is unrealistic.

A better approach:

Choose 2 platforms. And choose platforms you enjoy using as a consumer. If you love scrolling TikTok anyway, that's your platform. If you're naturally on LinkedIn for professional reasons, use that. If Instagram feels overwhelming or unfamiliar, don't force it. Your presence should ideally be rooted in genuine interest and aligned with your own preferences, not obligation.

Post 1-2 times per week and make your posts count. Align with your brand. Customize your posts to your persona readers (from Chapter 5) using messaging you know they'll connect with. Then enjoy the likes, comments, and shares that result from your efforts.

Use your 3-4 content pillars. You defined these in Chapter 8. Your content pillars are the categories or themes that organize everything you share publicly. They make content creation simpler because you always know what to talk about.

Build simple systems. Batch creation, templates, and repurposing make content creation efficient rather than time-consuming. You're not reinventing the wheel every time you post.

This approach might feel radically different from what you've been told. Most marketing advice assumes you have unlimited time and energy. You don't. Effective content strategy acknowledges this reality, leaving you time to do what you love - write.

The content that works best isn't the content that performs best in someone else's case study. It's the content you can create consistently without burning out.

It's easy to find yourself creating content that doesn't feel like you. The pressure is real: video platforms promise visibility, so you push yourself on camera even when it makes you uncomfortable. You've heard that a cheerful, upbeat voice performs well, so you cultivate one that doesn't match how you talk. Marketing advice says to post daily, so you drain your creative energy trying to keep up.

When content creation feels like performance instead of conversation, it's not because you're doing it wrong. It's because the strategy doesn't align with who you are.

Newsflash: You have the permission to choose the platforms you enjoy. Use your actual voice. Post at the frequency you can reasonably sustain.

This isn't lowering the bar – it's raising it. The only content strategy that works long-term is the one that's aligned with who you are.

WHY: Consistency Wins Every Time

Research on social media engagement shows that consistency matters more than volume. Accounts that post regularly (even just once or twice per week) with high-quality, on-brand content outperform accounts that post sporadically or flood feeds with content that doesn't resonate.

The Data: You might think posting more often is the answer to growing your audience. An analysis of over 21 million social media posts in 2025 reveals that engagement rates decline significantly when content frequency increases without strategic planning, proving that posting more doesn't mean performing better. Strategic presence and intentional content make the most impact.

Here's why effective content strategy works:

You maintain it. When your content strategy feels manageable, you stick with it. Consistency expands your effort, power, visibility and digital reach. A year of posting twice a week gives you 100+ touchpoints with your audience. That's powerful visibility—without burnout.

Your content quality improves. When you're not scrambling to post daily, you have time to create thoughtful content that serves your readers. You're not posting for the sake of posting. You're sharing content that aligns with your brand and connects with your persona readers.

You protect your capacity for other essential work. Content creation shouldn't consume all your promotional energy. You also need bandwidth for writing your next book, for direct outreach to bookstores and libraries, for speaking opportunities, for designing promotional materials. A realistic content strategy protects your capacity for everything else that matters.

Focus your energy on the activities that bring you the most meaning and fulfillment. If something isn't covered, you have options. Outsource it to someone on Fiverr or take a more radical approach—don't do it at all.

Don't apologize for what gets left off the list. Embrace and celebrate what you ARE doing. That self-appreciation will resonate with whatever audience you're cultivating on social media.

Consider a thriller author who initially tried to maintain Instagram, TikTok, Facebook, Twitter, and LinkedIn. She was posting 10+ times per week across platforms, spending 15+ hours on content creation, and feeling constantly behind. She felt guilty every time she opened social media. Her writing suffered, and she missed critical delivery deadlines. After six months, she was burned out and her book progress had stalled.

She stepped back and reassessed. She realized she enjoyed Twitter and found LinkedIn valuable for connecting with other authors and readers interested in true crime. She narrowed her focus to those two platforms. She committed to posting twice a week total—one thoughtful thread on Twitter, one article or insight on LinkedIn. Both aligned with her content pillars: criminal psychology, story craft, and the ethics of true crime storytelling.

Within three months, her engagement increased. Her writing productivity improved dramatically. She had energy for pitching podcast interviews and reaching out to bookstores. She felt in control rather than overwhelmed. Less became more.

Now consider a business author who tried to be on every platform, posting daily, creating reels and carousels and complex infographics. He spent 20 hours per week on content and hated every minute of it. Social media felt performative and draining.

Instead, he chose LinkedIn (where his corporate readers were) and committed to posting once per week—a single thoughtful post about leadership challenges his readers faced. That was it. One post per week aligned with his brand and his readers' needs.

His engagement tripled. His content sparked conversations. He had time and energy to pursue speaking opportunities at conferences. And he was writing again—because he wasn't spending half his available energy on something he didn't even enjoy.

The difference wasn't talent or effort. It was strategic simplicity.

HOW: Building Your Signature Content Strategy

Building a content strategy has three components: choosing your platforms, creating content from your pillars, and building systems that protect your time.

Choosing Your Platforms

You already audited your current platform presence in Chapter

11. Now you're making strategic decisions about where to focus.

Start with this question: What platforms do I enjoy most using as a consumer?

Not "What platforms should I be on?" Not "Where are all the authors?" But where do you naturally spend time? What platforms do you scroll through because you genuinely enjoy the content? That's your starting point.

If you love short-form videos and you're already on TikTok, that's a natural venue for you as a creator. If you're on LinkedIn for professional networking, creating content there makes sense. If you dread opening Instagram and it feels like a chore every time, that's a sign it's not your platform—even if other authors are finding success there.

Here's why this matters: Your presence needs to be rooted in genuine interest, not obligation. You might force yourself for a few weeks, maybe even a few months. But eventually, the friction will win. You'll post sporadically, feel guilty, and burn out. Choose platforms you like being on.

Next, cross-reference with your reader personas from Chapter 5. Where do your target readers spend the most time? If you write business books for executives and your readers are on LinkedIn, that's where you should be. If you write young adult fantasy and your readers are on TikTok and Instagram, choose one of those. Don't waste energy on platforms where your readers don't congregate.

Chapter 13 will guide you through deeper platform selection criteria and help you find your authentic voice on social media. For now, focus on the mechanics: pick platforms where your readers gather and you can create consistently.

Now narrow to two platforms. Not three. Not four. Two. This forces strategic focus. You're not trying to be everywhere—you're being intentional about where your energy is spent.

For most authors, one of those platforms should be an "owned channel"—your email newsletter. This is the one channel you control completely. Algorithms can't take it away. Platforms can't change the rules. Your email list is yours. If you're only choosing two platforms total and one is email, that means you're choosing one social platform. That's plenty.

Creating Content from Your Pillars

You defined your 3-4 content pillars in Chapter 8. Those pillars are the core themes that organize all your public-facing content. Now you're simply expressing those pillars in ways that fit your chosen platforms.

Let's say your content pillars are:

1. The craft of storytelling
2. The research process behind historical accuracy
3. Underrepresented histories you're passionate about
4. The author journey and creative process

These pillars give you endless content possibilities. You don't need to invent new topics every week—you're exploring different angles within your established themes.

On Twitter, this might look like:

- A thread about a surprising historical detail you discovered during research (Pillar 2)

- A reflection on balancing historical accuracy with narrative flow (Pillar 1)
- A recommendation for a lesser-known historical resource (Pillar 3)
- A candid post about navigating a challenging revision (Pillar 4)

On Instagram, this might look like:

- A carousel post showing your research process with archival photos (Pillar 2)
- A Reel discussing how you approach dialogue in historical fiction (Pillar 1)
- A post highlighting an underrepresented figure from history (Pillar 3)
- A behind-the-scenes photo from your writing space with a caption about your creative routine (Pillar 4)

Notice you're not creating completely different content for each platform. You're adapting your core themes to fit platform formats. The same research process that becomes a Twitter thread could become an Instagram carousel or a LinkedIn article. You're repurposing and adapting, not starting from scratch every time.

Your content should also connect to your persona readers. If your reader is a history teacher who values accuracy and classroom-ready resources, create content that speaks to her interests. Share primary source recommendations. Discuss how historical research informs your storytelling. Offer insights she can bring back to her students.

If your reader is a historical fiction reader who loves immersive, character-driven narratives, create content that shows your storytelling craft. Discuss character development.

Share how you balance historical detail with emotional resonance. Give him a window into your creative process.

You're not creating generic content. You're creating content your specific readers will care about.

These examples show what's possible with your content pillars. In Chapter 13, we'll dive deeper into how to make your content feel genuinely like you—how to engage authentically rather than perform, and how to build real relationships with readers.

Building Systems That Protect Your Time

Smart content strategy requires reflection, planning, and systems. Without systems, content creation becomes an endless, time-consuming grind. With systems, it becomes efficient, repeatable, and manageable.

Batch creation is your most powerful tool. Instead of creating content every time you need to post, set aside a few hours once or twice a month to create multiple pieces of content at once. Write 4-6 social media posts. Draft 2-3 email newsletters. Record several video clips if you're using video platforms. Then schedule them in advance.

Batching works because it reduces decision fatigue. When you sit down to create content in a batch session, you're in "content creation mode." You're not switching between writing, editing, content creation, email, admin work, and a dozen other tasks. You're focused, and that focus makes you more efficient.

Templates and frameworks make content creation faster. If you're posting on Instagram, create a visual template you can reuse—same fonts, same color palette, same layout structure. You're just swapping in new text and images. If you're writing

LinkedIn posts, develop a framework: open with a question or provocative statement, share a personal insight or story, bring in a metric or an expert opinion, close with a takeaway or invitation to engage. Once you have a structure, you're not reinventing the format every time.

Repurposing content multiplies your effort. A single idea can become multiple pieces of content adapted for different platforms. A blog post becomes a Twitter thread. A Twitter thread becomes an Instagram carousel. An email newsletter becomes a LinkedIn article. You're not creating 10 entirely new ideas—you're expressing one idea in 10 different ways.

Scheduling tools remove the burden of real-time posting. Use tools like Buffer, Hootsuite, Later, or platform-native scheduling features to queue up your content in advance. You create it once during your batch session, schedule it, and it posts automatically. You're not logging in daily to post. You're checking in to engage with comments and replies—which is far less time-intensive than content creation.

One caveat: don't let scheduling replace genuine engagement. Reserve time each week to actively engage with your followers' content—like their posts, leave comments, share posts that you feel your followers would also appreciate. This reciprocal engagement builds real connection and reminds your audience that there's a human behind your brand.

The goal of these systems isn't to automate away your presence or make your content feel robotic. The goal is to make content creation efficient enough that it doesn't consume your entire life. You want time and energy left for writing, for direct outreach, for the parts of your author journey that genuinely excite you.

CALIBRATION: Is Your Content Strategy Working?

Effective content strategy is working if you're maintaining it without burnout, building genuine engagement, and protecting energy for other essential work. You'll recognize the signs.

Warning Signs Your Strategy Needs Refinement:

✖ **You dread content creation.** If every time you sit down to create a post, you feel resistance or resentment, a change in approach is needed.

✖ **You're posting sporadically or inconsistently.** If you go weeks without posting, then try to catch up with a flurry of activity, then disappear again, your strategy needs adjustment.

✖ **Your writing is suffering.** If content creation is taking time away from your actual writing, your strategy is out of balance.

Indicators of Success:

✔ **You're posting consistently.** Whether it's once a week or twice a week, you're showing up regularly without it feeling like a burden.

✔ **You're enjoying the process.** You don't dread creating content. You might even look forward to it because you're sharing things you genuinely care about.

✔ **You have energy for other promotion work.** You're not spending all your time on content creation. You have capacity to reach out to bookstores, engage with book clubs, pursue speaking opportunities, and write your next book.

WORKROOM: Building Your Content Strategy

LEVEL 1: ESSENTIAL (Start Here) – 30 minutes

Identify your two platforms. One should be your email newsletter (your owned channel). The other should be a social platform you enjoy using as a consumer.

Choose one content pillar from Chapter 8. Brainstorm 4 different ways you could express that pillar on your chosen social platform. Don't write full posts—just jot down some ideas.

Set a recurring calendar reminder for one content creation session per month (1-2 hours). During that session, you'll batch create 4-8 pieces of content—enough for 1-2 posts per week for the next month.

Create your first post this week using one of the ideas you brainstormed.

Done. You now have a customized content strategy that doesn't require daily effort.

LEVEL 2: IF YOU WANT TO GO DEEPER

Map out a simple content calendar for the next month. Using your 3-4 content pillars, plan what you'll post each week. Alternate between pillars so your content feels varied.

Create templates for your chosen platform:

- If visual (Instagram, TikTok): Design a simple visual template with your brand colors and fonts
- If text-based (Twitter, LinkedIn): Develop 2-3 post frameworks you can reuse (e.g., question + insight + invitation to engage)

Schedule your first batch creation session. Set aside 2 hours. Create 6-8 pieces of content—social posts, email newsletter drafts, whatever fits your platforms. Use a scheduling tool to queue them up in advance.

Identify one piece of content you can repurpose across platforms. For example, take a blog post and turn it into a Twitter post, an Instagram carousel, and an email newsletter segment. Practice adapting one idea for multiple formats.

LEVEL 3: DEEP DIVE

Build a content library. Create a document or spreadsheet where you capture ideas as they come to you—interesting research discoveries, reader questions, thoughts about craft, behind-the-scenes moments. When it's time for your batch creation session, you already have a bank of ideas to pull from instead of starting from scratch.

Experiment with repurposing content systematically. For one month, take every piece of content you create and adapt it for at least two other formats or platforms. Track what formats get the best engagement.

Schedule quarterly content strategy reviews. Every 90 days, assess: What content got the strongest engagement? What felt most enjoyable to create? What felt like a drag? Adjust your approach based on what you learn.

Come back to this regularly. Your content strategy should evolve as your career grows and as your comfort level with different platforms changes.

This chapter gives you permission to do less—and do it better. The systems you've built here protect your time and energy for what matters: writing your next book and connecting meaningfully with readers. Next, we'll dive into how to engage authentically on social media without it feeling performative or exhausting—because showing up is only part of the equation. Connection is what makes it real.

CHAPTER 13

SOCIAL MEDIA WITH SOUL

Social media content creation shouldn't feel like a second job.

The authors who build genuine communities online aren't always the loudest voices or have the most followers. They show up as themselves, engage meaningfully with readers who resonate with their work, and approach social media as connection instead of obligation.

The value of social media isn't to be seen by everyone. It's to be recognized by the right people.

This chapter is about not only finding your voice but revealing it to your readers on platforms that matter to them, creating interactions that energize you, and building relationships that support your work for years—not just through a single book launch.

You already know how to connect with people. This chapter helps you do it strategically, sustainably, and in ways that feel good.

In Chapter 12, you built the systems that make content creation manageable—batching, templates, scheduling, and protecting your energy. You identified your platforms and established a realistic posting rhythm. Now we're digging deeper into the human element: to show up authentically on those platforms, to build genuine relationships with readers, and to engage in ways that energize rather than drain you.

WHAT: Authentic Presence

Showing up as yourself—not as the author you think you should be—creates genuine connection with readers who will love your work.

There's a fundamental difference between consuming social media content and creating it. When you're scrolling TikTok or Instagram on your break—watching videos, reading posts, enjoying what others share—that's leisure. But when you sit down to create content for those same platforms, you're doing work. Strategic work that requires thought, planning, creative energy, and skill.

Authentic social media presence means:

- Engaging consistently on platforms where your target readers spend time

- Sharing content that reflects your content pillars in your natural voice
- Balancing celebration of wins with genuine two-way engagement
- Building relationships with people who genuinely connect with your work
- Measuring success by engagement quality, not just follower quantity

Celebrating Wins Without Just Broadcasting

Of course you should share your wins—book releases, speaking gigs, awards, great reviews. These moments are precious, and your community genuinely wants to celebrate with you. But there's a way to share them that deepens connection rather than just broadcasts news.

Compare these approaches:

Broadcasting (one-way): "Excited to announce my book just won the XYZ Award! Link in bio."

Inviting conversation (two-way): "This morning I found out [Book Title] won the XYZ Award. Honestly? I'm thinking about all of you who beta-read early drafts, answered my panicked DMs about plot holes, and cheered me through revisions. Who are the people who've championed your creative work? Drop their names below and let's celebrate our champions together."

The first post shares news. The second shares news and creates connection—it acknowledges your community, invites them into the moment, and gives them space to share their own experiences. Both announce the win. Only one builds relationship.

Being Recognizably You

Think about the authors you follow online—the ones whose posts you read, whose content you engage with, whose books you buy. They're not the ones with the biggest followings or the slickest content. They're the ones who feel real, who share perspectives that resonate with you, who make you feel like you're part of a conversation rather than an audience.

Let's address the fear that stops most authors from showing up authentically on social media: the worry that their real personality is somehow unprofessional, inappropriate, or too much. Too serious. Too silly. Too political. Too emotional. Too opinionated. Too quiet. Too intense. Too weird. Here's the truth: The readers who need your book might be looking for exactly what you're afraid to reveal.

If you write dark psychological thrillers, readers aren't expecting sunshine and motivational quotes. If you write cozy mysteries, they're not looking for academic dissertation energy. If you write literary fiction exploring grief, your social media doesn't need to be relentlessly cheerful.

The alignment between who you are, what you write, and how you show up online isn't just authentic—it's strategic. It's how readers recognize you. It's how they decide you're their kind of author. You don't need to perform. You don't need to be "on" all the time. You don't need to adopt someone else's voice because it seems to work for them. You need to be recognizably, consistently you. That's not oversharing. That's branding.

When you show up as yourself—engaging your ME Factor—in ways that energize you, social media becomes a natural extension of who you are, how you express yourself, and how you promote your work.

WHY: Why Genuine Engagement Beats Performative Posting

Readers can tell the difference. And so can you.

The Data: Research shows that authentic content from real creators achieves 12x higher engagement rates than brand-generated sponsored content. Trust builds loyalty, and loyalty builds careers.

You attract the right readers, not just any readers. When you post content that genuinely reflects your interests and expertise on platforms where your target readers spend time, they don't just scroll past. They stop. They engage. They remember you. When your book releases, they're already familiar with your perspective and curious about your work. That's the strategic chain in action: targeted content builds familiarity, which sparks curiosity. Curiosity drives sales.

Generic promotional posts ask strangers to buy your book. Strategic promotion invites readers who already follow you to take the next step.

You build momentum. An author writes epic fantasy novels with intricate political systems. For months, he posted daily across four platforms—quotes, book covers, generic writing advice. His follower count grew slowly. His engagement was minimal. And he was exhausted.

Then he shifted. He narrowed his activity to Instagram and Twitter—and posted twice a week, focusing on his content pillars: worldbuilding craft, political theory in fantasy, the research behind his fictional governments. He engaged directly with fantasy fiction readers on Twitter, answering worldbuilding questions, sharing resources, participating in discussions. His follower count continued growing but his engagement increased by 60%. More importantly, he enjoyed it —conversations about things he cared about with people who shared his interests. When his book launched, those community members showed up. They bought, reviewed, and recommended.

Real engagement is energizing. Performative posting can feel meaningless, unfulfilling, and transactional.

You create advocates, not just audiences. Followers consume your content. Advocates share it, recommend your books, and show up for every release. You don't create advocates through follower counts—you create them through genuine connection.

Think about your reader personas. When you consistently share insights that matter to them, ask thoughtful questions about topics they care about, and engage meaningfully in their communities, they don't just follow you. They become advocates. They recommend your book to their networks. They show up for your launches. That's the magic of real connection.

When you engage in ways that feel natural on platforms you're genuinely drawn to, social media stops competing with your creative work and becomes part of the ecosystem that supports it.

This is permission to do less. Permission to show up as yourself. Permission to say no to platforms or posting frequencies. Success isn't about doing everything—it's about understanding what works for you and finding ways to enjoy the process.

HOW: Creating Real Connections on Social Media

Choose Platforms Based on Strategic Fit

Look at your reader personas. Where do they spend time? What platforms do they use for the type of content you want to share?

If your persona is a massage therapist who follows wellness practitioners on Instagram and TikTok, and you write about healing practices, those platforms make strategic sense for you. If your persona is a retired teacher who participates actively in Facebook book groups and Goodreads, those are your platforms.

Strategic fit means the intersection of where your readers are and where you can show up naturally. The whole process works better if you're genuinely drawn to that platform and enjoy the content on it—even as a consumer. If you hate video content, TikTok won't work no matter how many readers are there. If long-form writing energizes you, LinkedIn or Medium might be perfect even if they're not the trendiest options.

Both elements matter: where your readers are and where you can sustainably create content.

Define Your Voice

Your voice on social media should sound like you talking to a friend about something you care about. Not you performing. Not you copying what works for other authors. The real you.

This doesn't mean unprofessional. It means honest. Your voice might be warm and conversational, thoughtful and analytical, funny and irreverent, earnest and passionate, or quiet and contemplative. All of these work. What doesn't work is forcing yourself into a voice that isn't yours.

Test this: Read your recent posts out loud. Do they sound like something you'd say? Or do they sound like you're reading from a marketing script? If it's the latter, readers can tell.

Your voice should align with your brand through-line. If your books deliver "empowered clarity to create effective change," your social media voice might be direct, encouraging, and solution-focused. If your novels deliver "justice served with compassion for human complexity," your voice might be thoughtful, nuanced, and empathetic.

This isn't about creating a character. It's about letting yourself show up as yourself.

Use Your Content Pillars to Stay Focused

Your content pillars guide not just what you post but what conversations you engage in. If one of your pillars is "the intersection of science and spirituality" (you write speculative fiction exploring consciousness), you know exactly which posts to comment on, which discussions to join, which content to share.

This clarity keeps you on track. You're not trying to engage with everything—you're engaging strategically with content that aligns with your brand and genuinely interests you.

Sarah writes historical romance set in the Victorian era. Her content pillars include historical research and accuracy, women's agency in constrained societies, and the craft of writing romance. Every post, comment, and engagement connects to one of these pillars. She doesn't chase trending topics unless they intersect with her pillars. She doesn't force herself to comment on posts outside her areas of genuine interest. She's not everywhere. But where she is, she's visible, recognized, remembered, and valued.

More Engaging. Less Broadcasting.

Real engagement looks like:

Commenting meaningfully on others' posts. This can be as simple as "Great post!" or "Thanks for sharing!" when something resonates—brief engagement is better than no engagement. When you have more to offer, take a moment to add perspective, ask thoughtful questions, or share relevant experience. If someone posts about worldbuilding challenges in fantasy and that intersects with your content pillars, share your perspective. Tell a story about a worldbuilding problem you solved in one of your books. Ask a question that deepens the conversation.

Responding genuinely to comments on your posts. When someone comments, they've given you their attention. Honor that. Respond with substance. Ask follow-up questions. Create actual dialogue. This is how followers become community members.

Sharing others' content. When you find content that aligns with your pillars and serves your readers, share it. Credit the creator and add your perspective on why it matters. This positions you as a connector and curator, not just a promoter.

Being present in communities. Join the Facebook groups, Goodreads groups, or Instagram communities where your readers gather. Participate genuinely. Answer questions. Share resources. Be helpful. Don't show up just to promote your book —show up because you're genuinely part of the community.

Think about social media as a coffee shop, not a billboard. You're there to have conversations with interesting people, not to shout announcements at strangers.

Create Content That Invites Engagement

The best posts do three things: they connect to your content pillars, they invite perspective or participation, and they sound like you.

Instead of: "Writers: what's your word count today?" Try: "I'm working on a scene where my character has to choose between loyalty and truth. It's the kind of scene that makes me question my own values while I write. Do you ever find your characters forcing you to examine your own beliefs?"

This invites deeper conversation and reveals something real about your process.

Instead of: "My book releases next month! Here's the cover!" Try: "I spent three years researching Victorian medical practices for this novel. The most surprising thing I learned: [specific, interesting detail]. What's the most unexpected thing you've learned while researching a historical period?"

This connects to your pillar, invites engagement, and shares something genuinely interesting.

The best content invites response. It asks questions, shares perspectives, creates space for others to be heard.

Measure What Matters

Meaningful metrics include:

- **Quality engagement:** Comments that show people who read your post. Shares. Direct messages from readers who connect with your work.
- **Community growth:** People who show up consistently, engage regularly, and know your name and work.
- **Conversion to readers:** Website clicks, newsletter signups, book sales from your social media community.
- **Your own sustainability:** Do you enjoy creating content on this platform? Does it energize or drain you?

If you have 500 followers and 50 of them engage meaningfully with your posts, recommend your books to their networks, and show up for your releases, you have a more valuable platform than 10,000 followers who passively scroll past your content.

Quality beats quantity. Always.

Protect Your Boundaries

You get to decide how often you post, which platforms you use, what you share and what you don't, how much time you spend engaging, and what conversations you participate in.

Real social media presence doesn't mean being available 24/7 or responding to every comment within minutes or participating in every conversation or trend.

You show up consistently in ways that work for you and engage genuinely, leaving time and space for what matters most.

This is permission to opt out. To log off. To say no. Because the goal isn't to be everywhere—it's to be genuinely present where you are.

CALIBRATION: Is Your Social Media Working?

Warning Signs:

✗ **You dread posting.** If social media feels like obligatory, something's misaligned. Either the platforms aren't right for you, your content doesn't reflect your natural voice, or you're forcing yourself to meet an unrealistic posting schedule. Step back and ask: what would make this feel energizing instead of draining?

✗ **Your engagement is mostly promotional.** If your posts get likes but no meaningful comments, if your followers don't respond to your questions, you're broadcasting instead of engaging. Shift from announcements to invitations.

✗ **You're performing a voice that isn't yours.** If you find yourself copying other authors' styles, using language that doesn't feel natural, or posting content you don't genuinely care about, readers will feel the disconnect.

If you're seeing these signs, that's okay. Reconnect with your content pillars. Remember who you're trying to reach and where they are. Give yourself permission to be more intentional about your engagement.

Indicators of Success:

✔ **Your posts create conversations.** People don't just like—they comment meaningfully. They ask questions. They share their own perspectives. You're not posting into the void; you're creating dialogue with people who care about the same things you do.

✔ **Readers recognize you across interactions.** People remember your name, your books, your perspective. They mention seeing your posts. They reference conversations you've had. You're becoming familiar, recognizable, memorable—exactly what you need from social media.

✔ **You enjoy engaging.** You get a clever idea for a specific type of post and you're excited about creating. If you're having fun with it, you've found your rhythm and your connections will see that.

You've got this. Real engagement isn't about doing more—it's about being more intentionally yourself.

WORKROOM: Building Real Engagement

LEVEL 1: ESSENTIAL (Start here) – 30 minutes

Pick a platform, review your last 10 social media posts and your responses to comments:

- Read them aloud. Do they sound like you talking to a friend? Circle the ones that feel natural and note what makes them different.
- Look at which posts got meaningful engagement (comments, not just likes). What do those posts have in common?
- Check your comment responses. Are you creating

dialogue or just thanking people? Choose one post from this week and respond to comments with follow-up questions or added perspective.

Based on what you notice, write down: "My voice sounds most like me when I..." and "Posts that create real engagement tend to..."

LEVEL 2: IF YOU WANT TO GO DEEPER *(Optional)*

Audit your current social media presence:

- List the communities where your target readers gather. Join one you're not already part of and observe for a week before engaging.
- Map your recent posts to your content pillars. What percentage connect clearly to your pillars? What percentage are off-brand or reactive?
- Track your engagement quality for two weeks. Count meaningful comments, new connections with readers in your target audience, direct messages about your work, and moments when you enjoyed the interaction.

What are your audit results? You can adjust your content based on what creates genuine connection.

LEVEL 3: DEEP DIVE *(Come back to this over weeks/months)*

Build a systematic approach to meaningful engagement:

- Create a simple engagement plan: which 3-5 types of posts create the most meaningful dialogue? Draft templates that maintain your natural voice while inviting engagement.

- Identify 2-3 people in your target reader community who consistently engage meaningfully. Make it a practice to genuinely engage with their content weekly—not for exposure, but because their perspectives align with your interests.
- Experiment with one platform or engagement type you've been avoiding. Give it four weeks of honest effort. If it still doesn't feel energizing, give yourself permission to drop it permanently.

The goal isn't to be everywhere or to engage perfectly. It's to build meaningful relationships and enjoy the process.

CHAPTER 14
CRACK THE AMAZON CODE

Amazon is a discovery engine waiting to work for you.

Every day, millions of readers search Amazon for their next book. They type specific phrases into the search bar. They browse categories. They read descriptions to see if a book promises what they're looking for. When your Amazon presence is strategically optimized, those readers find you. When it's not, they find someone else.

The good news? You already have everything you need to optimize your Amazon presence: your reader personas, your content pillars, your strategic positioning. This chapter shows you how to translate those insights into Amazon's language: keywords, categories, book descriptions, and A+ Content—so readers actively searching for books like yours can find them. A+ Content is Amazon's enhanced content feature that lets you add rich graphics and formatted text to your book page, creating a more compelling brand presence and a more memorable experience for potential readers.

Amazon isn't complicated. It's systematic. And once you understand the system, you can make it work for you 24/7.

WHAT: Amazon as a Strategic Platform

Amazon is a system powered by algorithms that match books with readers based on keywords, categories, and reader behavior. Your job is to give Amazon's algorithm the information it needs to connect your book with the right readers.

Think of Amazon as a sophisticated recommendation engine. When a reader searches for "organizational change management" or browses the "Business Leadership" category, Amazon's algorithm decides which books to show them. Those decisions are based on metadata you provide: your keywords, your categories, your book description, your A+ Content.

Amazon is the first place readers go to learn about books, research them, and make purchasing decisions. Your Amazon book page isn't just a sales channel—it's your strategic storefront. It's the welcome mat for potential readers. It's the door to your long-term sales pipeline.

When your Amazon presence is optimized, you're not just improving one aspect of your author platform. You're strengthening a critical discovery and sales pathway.

Every piece of information you give Amazon—every keyword, every category choice, every phrase in your book description—is an opportunity to be discovered by the right readers who are actively searching for what you write.

But here's where the real power multiplies: You might have an author platform spanning multiple sites—website, social media channels, blog, newsletter. When those platforms all speak the same language, use the same strategic keywords, and reinforce the same brand message, they amplify each other. The wires touch—and that's where the magic spark happens. Amazon helps create that alignment because it requires you to be precise and strategic about who your book is for and what makes it unique.

Your Amazon optimization isn't separate from your author brand—it's an extension of it.

WHY: Amazon Optimization Matters

Discoverability means when readers search Amazon for books in your category, they find you—not your competition.

The Data: Amazon accounts for 50% of all U.S. book sales and 83% of the e-book market. This means more than half of all readers in the United States will discover and purchase your book through Amazon—making your Amazon presence the single most critical piece of your book marketing infrastructure, author platform, and brand visibility. Your Amazon author page, book descriptions, categories, and reviews aren't just sales tools—they're the primary way most readers will form their first impression of you as an author.

And this type of discoverability isn't luck. It's communication. When your metadata clearly communicates who your book is for and what makes it unique, Amazon's algorithm can connect you with readers who want exactly what you write.

Search and browsing drive discovery. When someone searches "data-driven decision making for executives," Amazon shows them books whose metadata matches that search. If your business book on leveraging analytics for strategic leadership appears in those results, it's because your keywords, categories, and description told Amazon's algorithm that your book delivers what that reader is seeking.

Your reader personas are on Amazon right now, searching for their next read. They're using specific phrases, browsing specific categories, reading book descriptions. Strategic optimization means speaking their language so they can find you.

Categories create visibility pathways. Amazon allows you to choose up to 3 categories for your book through your KDP dashboard. Each category is a pathway for readers to discover your book through browsing.

Strategic category selection means finding where your target readers browse and where you can realistically rank. A Top 100 placement in a well-chosen subcategory means your book appears on the first page when readers browse that category—visibility that grows over time.

Keywords bridge reader intent and your book. Amazon allows seven keyword phrases (up to 50 characters each). These aren't visible to readers, but they tell Amazon's algorithm when to show your book in search results and recommendations.

If your reader persona searches "workplace culture transformation strategies," and your keywords include those phrases, Amazon knows to show your book. The connection happens. The reader searching for exactly what you wrote sees your book because your metadata did its job by communicating the match.

Book descriptions convert browsers to buyers. Your book description does three things: connects emotionally with your target reader, promises the experience they're seeking, and gives them enough compelling detail to click "buy." When you incorporate your keywords naturally, speak directly to your reader personas, and align with your brand through-line, your description becomes a conversion tool.

A+ Content amplifies your brand. Amazon A+ Content (available to authors enrolled in KDP or who have a publisher using Vendor Central) lets you add rich images and formatted text to your book's product page. The real power isn't just the graphics—it's in the metadata and text that accompanies those images. Every module is another opportunity to reinforce your keywords, speak to your reader personas, and create a memorable brand experience.

When your A+ Content, book description, keywords, and categories all align with your content pillars and reader personas, you're creating a cohesive brand experience. That alignment means all your platforms amplify each other rather than existing in isolation.

Reviews and ratings build social proof. Amazon prominently displays your book's star rating and number of reviews. Books with strong review counts and ratings of 4+ stars build reader trust and can benefit from increased visibility as the algorithm recognizes genuine customer engagement. You can make it easy for satisfied readers to leave reviews by including a polite request in your book's back matter and following up with readers on your email list.

When optimization works, readers discover your book through search, browsing, and Amazon's recommendation engine. They read your strategically crafted description, see social proof through reviews, and make a purchase. Then Amazon's algorithm notices that readers who liked certain books also liked yours—and starts recommending you to more readers.

That's the effect of strategic optimization.

HOW: Make Amazon Work for You

Research Your Strategic Keywords

Start with your reader personas and content pillars. What specific phrases would your target readers search for when looking for their next book?

Go to Amazon and start typing relevant phrases into the search bar. Amazon's autocomplete suggestions show you what real readers are searching for. If you write about workplace innovation, type "innovation leadership" and note what Amazon suggests: "innovation leadership books," "leading innovation teams," "innovation strategy." These are phrases real readers use.

If you write historical mysteries, type '1849 San Francisco mystery' and note what Amazon suggests: 'gold rush detective,' 'California historical mystery,' 'frontier crime fiction.' These autocomplete suggestions reveal the exact phrases readers in your genre have used when searching.

Look at your comp titles—the 5-6 books you identified in your market intelligence work. What keywords appear repeatedly in their book descriptions? What categories are they in? What phrases show up in their top reviews? Patterns reveal the language your target readers use.

Use Amazon's search results to understand competition. Search for potential keyword phrases and note how many results appear. "Leadership" yields millions of results—highly competitive. "Leading remote teams through change" yields thousands—more specific, less competitive, better for targeted discovery.

Create a list of 15-20 strategic keyword phrases that your target readers would search for. Prioritize phrases that balance specificity (reaching your exact readers) with searchability (the phrases readers use).

Choose Your Categories Strategically

Browse Amazon's category structure to understand where your book naturally fits and where your target readers browse. The subcategories often provide better visibility than top-level categories.

A business book on organizational change management could fit in:

- Business & Money > Management & Leadership > Organizational Change
- Business & Money > Human Resources > Workplace Culture
- Business & Money > Management & Leadership > Strategic Planning
- Self-Help > Personal Transformation

Or a historical mystery set during the San Francisco gold rush could fit in:

- Mystery, Thriller & Suspense > Mystery > Historical
- Literature & Fiction > Historical Fiction
- Literature & Fiction > Genre Fiction > Historical

Each category is a different pathway for discovery. Choose categories where:

1. Your target readers browse
2. The top books in that category are similar to yours (you belong there)
3. You can realistically achieve Top 100 ranking

Through your Amazon KDP (Kindle Direct Publishing) dashboard, select your 3 categories strategically. This gives you 3 pathways for readers to discover your book through browsing.

Craft a Strategic Book Description

Your book description connects emotionally with your target reader in the first two sentences, promises the experience they're seeking, and gives them enough detail to click buy.

Structure your description in three parts:

- **Hook (2-3 sentences):** Open with a question, provocative statement, or scenario that speaks directly to your reader persona's desires.
- **Promise (1-2 paragraphs):** Describe what the reader will experience—the emotional journey, the stakes, the core conflict. Incorporate your strategic keywords

naturally. Connect to your emotional promise and brand through-line.

- **Details (1 paragraph):** Give just enough plot or content detail to create curiosity. For fiction, hint at the central conflict and stakes. For nonfiction, outline what the reader will learn or achieve.

Fiction example for a gold rush mystery:

What if the fortune you came west to find was the one thing that would destroy you?

In the fog-choked streets of 1849 San Francisco, where gold fever has turned men into gamblers and killers, one murder should have been simple to solve.

Former Boston constable Daniel MacKenzie abandoned his badge and his past to start fresh in California's boomtown. But when a prospector is found dead in an alley behind the Golden Gate Saloon—his pockets empty, his claim papers missing— Daniel is pulled back into the work he swore he'd left behind.

The victim wasn't just another unlucky miner. He'd discovered something in the hills that made powerful men nervous—and now those men want Daniel to stop asking questions.

As Daniel digs deeper, he uncovers a web of claim jumping, forged deeds, and murders disguised as frontier accidents. The fortune beneath California's soil has created a new kind of criminal—one who operates behind lawyers and land offices, not six-guns and masks.

But this case isn't just about justice anymore. The men behind these crimes know about Daniel's past—the reason he fled Boston, the secret he's been running from. And they're willing to expose it unless he walks away.

This time, the cost of truth isn't just his reputation.

It's everything.

Atmospheric, morally complex, and rich with period detail, [Book Title] delivers a gripping mystery where gold dust and blood mix in the muddy streets of America's most lawless city— and where doing the right thing might cost you everything you came west to find.

"A taut, intelligent historical mystery with authentic grit" - [Publication]

Notice how this description hooks immediately with a compelling question, promises atmospheric period detail, incorporates keywords naturally (1849 San Francisco, claim jumping, California boomtown, historical mystery), and ends with social proof from an editorial review.

Nonfiction example for a business book on organizational change strategies:

Why do 70% of organizational change initiatives fail—even when the strategy is sound?

The answer isn't better planning or stronger leadership. It's understanding that resistance isn't the enemy of change—it's information you're not listening to.

This book provides a proven framework for leading transformation that builds on how people process change, not how we wish they would. You'll learn how to diagnose the real barriers to adoption (hint: it's rarely what leadership thinks), engage skeptics without forcing compliance, and create sustainable change capacity that outlasts any single initiative. Whether you're leading a digital transformation, restructuring operations, or implementing new systems, this approach works across industries and organization sizes.

Drawing on neuroscience, systems thinking, and case studies from Fortune 500 companies to mid-sized manufacturers, you'll discover practical tools for turning resistance into partnership, designing change processes that stick, and measuring what matters. You'll walk away with a field-tested methodology that addresses the human dynamics traditional change management ignores—and a clear roadmap for implementation starting Monday morning.

For leaders tired of watching good strategies fail because of "people problems," this book reframes the challenge entirely: people aren't the problem. They're the solution you haven't engaged yet.

"A rare combination of practical wisdom and psychological insight that fundamentally shifts how leaders approach organizational transformation." – [Publication]

This description hooks immediately with a compelling question, promises practical tools and field-tested methodology, incorporates keywords naturally (organizational change, digital transformation, leading transformation, change management), and ends with social proof from an editorial review.

Read your description out loud. Does it sound like you? Does it speak to your target reader? Does it naturally incorporate your strategic keywords? Revision is part of the process.

Optimize Your Author Central Profile

Claim your Amazon Author Central account (authorcentral.amazon.com). This is where you control your author bio, upload your author photo, add editorial reviews, and manage your book catalog.

Your author bio should align with your brand positioning and content pillars. Tell readers what you write about, why you write it, and what experience they can expect from your work. Incorporate relevant keywords naturally.

Upload a professional author photo that matches what you use across all platforms. Add your website URL and link to your other books.

Use the editorial reviews section to add early reviews, endorsements, or accolades. Social proof builds trust.

Implement Amazon A+ Content

If you're enrolled in Amazon KDP (or working with a publisher using Vendor Central), you have access to A+ Content—a tool that lets you create a richer book page experience.

A+ Content allows you to add:

- Custom images and graphics
- Comparison charts (excellent for series)
- Author bios with photos

- Additional book details
- Brand storytelling modules

The real power is in the text and metadata that accompanies the visuals. Each module you add is another opportunity to:

- Reinforce your strategic keywords
- Speak directly to your reader personas
- Create a cohesive brand experience
- Differentiate your book

For example, you might create an A+ module showing your series in reading order with short descriptions of each book (incorporating keywords). Or a module explaining your unique approach to your topic (for nonfiction). Or "What readers are saying" featuring compelling review quotes that speak to your emotional promise.

A+ Content creates a richer, more memorable experience on your book's product page. It also keeps readers on your page longer, which signals to Amazon's algorithm that your page is engaging—potentially boosting your visibility.

Build Social Proof Through Reviews

Amazon's algorithm favors books with more reviews and higher ratings. While you can't buy reviews or incentivize them (Amazon's terms of service prohibit this), you can make it easy for genuine readers to leave them.

Include a polite request in your book's back matter: "If you enjoyed this book, I'd be grateful if you'd leave a review on Amazon. Reviews help readers discover books they'll love."

Send a follow-up email to your newsletter subscribers a week or two after they've had time to read. Thank them for reading and gently remind them that reviews help other readers discover your work.

Focus on writing books that genuinely deliver on your emotional promise—satisfied readers leave reviews organically.

Create Platform Alignment

In Chapter 11, you audited your platform for visual and brand consistency—ensuring your profile pictures, positioning statements, and voice felt cohesive across channels. Now we're taking that alignment deeper: making sure your platforms use the same strategic keywords you've identified for Amazon optimization.

Review all your platform sites: your website, social media profiles, newsletter sign-up page, blog. Are they using the same strategic keywords you've identified for Amazon? Is your positioning consistent across all platforms?

If your Amazon keywords include "strategic leadership workplace culture" but your website never mentions those phrases, you're missing an alignment opportunity. If your LinkedIn bio describes you differently than your Amazon author bio, readers moving between platforms experience a disconnect.

Strategic alignment means using your keywords consistently, maintaining your brand voice across platforms, and ensuring that a reader who discovers you on Amazon and then visits your website has a cohesive experience. They should recognize you immediately. That recognition builds trust and memorability.

This is where the "spark" happens—when all your platforms speak the same language and amplify the same message, readers remember your brand. Amazon provides the structure to clarify that message, and your other platforms reinforce it.

CALIBRATION: Is Your Amazon Optimization Working?

Warning Signs:

✖ **Your book isn't appearing in relevant searches.** If you search for phrases your target readers would use and your book doesn't appear in the first several pages of results, your keywords and categories need adjustment. Research what phrases readers search for and revise your metadata.

✖ **Your category rankings aren't giving you visibility.** If you're ranked #50,000 in "Books" but not ranking in any specific subcategories, your categories aren't strategically selected. You need visibility in categories where your target readers browse.

✖ **Readers aren't converting after visiting your page.** If your book page gets traffic (visible in your KDP dashboard) but you're seeing few purchases, your book description isn't effectively communicating your value to your target readers. It might not speak to their specific desires or incorporate the emotional promise they're seeking.

If you're seeing these warning signs, that's useful information. Go back to your reader personas. What language do they use? What are they searching for? What emotional experience are they seeking? Let those insights guide your revisions.

Indicators of Success:

✔ **Your book appears in relevant search results.** When you search for phrases your target readers would use, your book appears in the first few pages of results. Even better, Amazon recommends your book when readers view comp titles. Your metadata is effectively communicating to Amazon's algorithm who your book is for.

✔ **Your category rankings give you visibility.** You're achieving Top 100 (ideally Top 20) rankings in several well-chosen subcategories where your target readers browse. This visibility translates directly to organic discovery.

✔ **Your page converts browsers into buyers.** Readers who land on your book's page frequently make a purchase. Your description effectively communicates your value, your reviews provide social proof, and your A+ Content creates a compelling brand experience. You're not just getting traffic—you're converting it.

Amazon optimization is about communicating clearly with readers who are actively looking for books exactly like yours. When you do that well, Amazon's discovery engine works for you.

WORKROOM: Optimizing Your Amazon Presence

LEVEL 1: ESSENTIAL (Start here) – 30 minutes

Focus on keywords and categories:

- Brainstorm 20 keyword phrases your target readers

would search for. Use Amazon's search bar autocomplete feature to see examples of real searches.

- Search those phrases and note how many results appear. Highlight 7 phrases that balance specificity with searchability.
- Input those 7 keyword phrases into your KDP dashboard (or update existing keywords).
- Browse Amazon's category structure and identify 3 categories where your target readers browse and where you could realistically rank in the Top 100. Update your categories through your KDP dashboard.

This foundation immediately improves your discoverability.

LEVEL 2: IF YOU WANT TO GO DEEPER *(Optional)*

Optimize your book description and Author Central profile:

- Review your current book description. Does it speak directly to your target reader in the first two sentences? Does it naturally incorporate your strategic keywords? Does it promise the emotional experience your readers seek?
- Rewrite your description using the Hook-Promise-Details structure. Read it out loud. Would your target reader persona feel compelled to buy?
- Claim your Author Central account if you haven't already. Update your bio to align with your brand positioning and naturally incorporate relevant keywords.
- Add editorial reviews or endorsements if you have them.

This deeper optimization takes 1-2 hours and significantly improves conversion.

LEVEL 3: DEEP DIVE *(Come back to this over weeks/months)*

Implement A+ Content and platform alignment:

- If you're enrolled in KDP, create A+ Content for each of your published books. Plan 3-5 modules that showcase your book, reinforce your keywords, create a memorable brand experience and compelling visuals for readers.
- Audit all your platform sites (website, social media, newsletter) for keyword and positioning consistency. Are you using the same strategic keywords across all platforms? Is your brand voice consistent?
- Create a simple spreadsheet tracking your category rankings weekly. Notice patterns: which categories drive the most visibility? Which need adjustment?
- Monitor which search terms drive traffic to your book page (visible in your KDP dashboard). Study what's working.

This comprehensive approach takes time but creates the platform alignment that generates evidence that all your platforms amplify each other and work together to build your author brand.

The goal isn't perfection. It's strategic clarity that connects your book with readers actively searching for what you wrote.

PART VI

HUMAN CONNECTION: BEYOND THE SCREEN

Beyond the laptop screen lies the irreplaceable power of human connection: conversations that build advocates, presence that builds trust, and self-care that sustains your career.

In this section, debut authors will learn how to leverage the power of bookstores, libraries, speaking opportunities, and media presence to multiply your reach beyond digital platforms.

Published authors will add the missing piece: in-person relationships. You'll learn how to build partnerships with booksellers, librarians, and event organizers who hand-sell your work to readers who trust them.

Returning authors will reconnect with the parts of author life that matter most—real conversations, authentic visibility, and sustainable practices that protect your creative energy long-term.

CHAPTER 15

HUMAN CONNECTION: MARKETING'S MISSING LINK

You spend your days in invisible spaces.

You write alone. You market to algorithms. You email strangers and post into the void of social media, hoping someone—anyone—sees it. Your book exists as pixels on screens, metadata in databases, a fleeting image rolling past in an endless feed.

And then you walk into a bookstore, hold a physical copy of your book, and hand it to a real person who says, "Tell me about this."

That moment—that actual human conversation about the story

you brought into the world—changes everything.

This chapter isn't about efficiency or scale. It's about broadening your network of advocates who genuinely care about the stories you're bringing into the world and see their value. Booksellers and librarians aren't just gatekeepers—they're readers who care deeply about human perspectives, about deepening conversations, about building awareness of voices that matter. When they connect with your work, they bring it into their communities with an enthusiasm and credibility you can't manufacture online.

When so much of our waking energy is spent in invisible, digital spaces, efficiency starts to make the world feel meaningless. It's the power of actual human connection that brings us back to ourselves and to each other. And bookstores and libraries are where that magic happens.

WHAT: Standing in Your ME Factor

Remember your ME Factor from Chapter 2? Your Goal + Audience + YOU = Your unique positioning in the market. You've refined it, tested it, built your entire author brand around it. You know what makes your work different. You understand the emotional promise you deliver to readers.

Now imagine standing face-to-face with a bookseller or librarian and articulating that with confidence and pride.

This is where your ME Factor changes from a strategy to conversation. It becomes the story of why your book matters, told by you, to someone who might become your advocate. When you can look someone in the eye and say, "Here's what this book does for readers that nothing else does quite this way," you're not just pitching. You're inviting someone into the world you've created.

Most authors find this terrifying at first. Speaking about your own work, explaining its value without apologizing or minimizing, being excited rather than self-deprecating—these don't come naturally to everyone. But this skill is learnable, and bookstore and library outreach gives you low-stakes opportunities to practice. Every conversation makes the next one easier.

The gift of physical presence is this: you get to be a human being talking about something you care about, not just a name on a cover. And the person across from you gets to see your passion, your authenticity, your genuine belief in what you've created. That connection—that transfer of enthusiasm—is something no amount of digital marketing can replicate.

Bookstores and libraries aren't just places that stock books—they're curated ecosystems where readers trust the people behind the recommendations. When a bookseller hand-sells your book to a customer, that customer may be far more likely to buy it, read it, and recommend it to their friends or family. When a librarian recommends your book in their monthly newsletter or adds it to a book club reading list, they're lending their credibility to your work.

The distinction that matters: there's a difference between having your book *stocked* and having your book *recommended*. Strategic outreach builds toward recommendation through genuine human connection.

WHY: The Multiplier Effect of Advocacy

The Data: Physical bookstores continue to drive discovery and account for a significant portion of book sales, while library digital checkouts hit a record 739 million in 2024—a 17% increase showing libraries remain vital to reader engagement. These aren't casual browsers—they're committed readers constantly hungry for their next book.

But the real power isn't in those statistics. It's in what happens when someone talks about your book with genuine enthusiasm.

When a bookseller becomes an advocate for your work, several things can manifest in ways you can't predict:

Word-of-mouth momentum: A customer buys your book based on a trusted recommendation. If they enjoy it, they may tell their friends, their coworkers, post on social media, and leave a review. That single hand-sell has power that advertising will never match.

Community reach: One bookstore relationship could lead to a book club invitation. That book club could include a librarian who adds your books to three additional library branches, bringing your book and your name more reach and visibility. Those library patrons may leave reviews, recommend your book to friends, and show up to your next book signing event.

Local media opportunities: Bookstores and libraries often have relationships with local media. An in-store event could lead to local newspaper coverage, radio interviews, or podcast features—all of which amplify your visibility beyond that single event.

Long-term credibility: Being featured in a bookstore's staff picks or a library's newsletter signals quality and credibility to readers. It's third-party validation that can build trust.

Example: A debut fantasy author cultivated relationships with three independent bookstores in her region. When her novel released, all three stores featured it in their staff picks and hosted small launch events. One of those events led to a local newspaper interview. Six months later, one of those booksellers recommended her novel to their book club, which included a speaking opportunity. That book club included a librarian who added the novel to her library's collection and invited the author to their annual author event. One relationship created a cascading series of opportunities.

Example: A career coach published a book on job search strategies. She approached a Barnes & Noble community relations coordinator and offered to host a free workshop on resume writing for their customers. The event drew 30 attendees, sold 15 books that evening, and resulted in the store stocking additional copies. The community relations coordinator later recommended her as a speaker for a regional business conference. That initial bookstore partnership opened doors far beyond book sales.

This isn't about mass distribution—it's about strategic relationship-building that can have lasting effects on your writing career. But more than that, it's about finding people who see the value in what you've created and want to share it with others. That kind of advocacy—rooted in genuine enthusiasm—is marketing's missing link.

Beyond the visibility and reach this kind of advocacy creates, direct person-to-person outreach has other significant advantages. It builds your confidence and public speaking skills. It helps you cultivate self-appreciation for your writing ability and career success. Every time you articulate why your book matters to someone who's listening with genuine interest, you're reinforcing your own belief in your work. That confidence carries into every other aspect of your brand and your career.

HOW: Building Genuine Partnerships Through Conversation

Effective bookstore and library outreach begins with research, but it's sustained through authentic human connection. Here's how to approach it strategically:

Research before you reach out

Identify 8-10 bookstores in your home region—places you've visited before. This gives you a significant advantage when you follow up your pitch letter with an in-person visit, telling them you love their store and shop there often.

Include both independent bookstores and major chains like Barnes & Noble. Visit their websites and social media. What kinds of books do they feature? Do they host author events? Do they have a book club? What's their community focus?

For chain bookstores, identify the community relations coordinator or store manager. Call the store directly and ask who handles author events and local partnerships.

For libraries, identify 3-5 library systems in your area. Tip: Visit the library first and get a library card in your name before you pitch. Being able to share that you use their library system personally creates credibility and connection, showing you're already part of their community. Find the name and contact information for the acquisitions librarian or programming coordinator.

Craft your pitch with partnership in mind

Your pitch should be concise, personalized, and focused on partnership. Include a keyword-rich book synopsis that mirrors your Amazon description, state who your key audience segments are, include comparable titles that share DNA with your work, and emphasize what you can offer their community through events or workshops.

The templates below give you concrete starting points you can adapt to your own work:

Example: Bookstore Pitch Letter

Subject: [Book Title] — New Crime Thriller & Author Event Opportunity

Dear [Bookseller/Events Coordinator Name],

I hope this message finds you well! My name is [Your Name], and I'm thrilled to introduce my latest crime thriller, [Book Title]. I wanted to reach out to see if [Bookstore Name] would be interested in stocking copies and possibly hosting an author event.

Synopsis: [Book Title] follows detective Emma Russo as she returns to her hometown of Ridgewood to settle her late father's estate—only to discover he was investigating a decades-old disappearance before his sudden death. When Emma begins asking questions, she uncovers a web of corruption involving the town's most powerful families, a pattern of silenced witnesses, and evidence that suggests her father's death was no accident. Racing against those who want the past buried, Emma must decide how far she'll go to expose the truth.

Comparative Titles: Fans of Tana French's *In the Woods* and William Kent Krueger's *Ordinary Grace* will recognize a shared DNA in [Book Title]—a small-town mystery where the past refuses to stay buried, family secrets run deep, and one determined investigator risks everything for justice.

I would love to collaborate with [Bookstore Name] on an author signing, reading, or virtual Q&A, bringing this story directly to readers and creating a memorable experience for your community. I can provide advance copies, promotional materials, and social media assets to support the event.

My book is distributed through Ingram [and returns are accepted, if applicable], and my Author Media Kit is attached for your review.

Please let me know the best contact person for event inquiries or ordering copies. I'd be delighted to work with you to bring [Book Title] to your readers.

Thank you so much for your time and consideration. I look forward to connecting!

Warm regards, [Your Name] [Your contact information] [Your website]

Example: Library Pitch Letter

Subject: [Book Title] — New Crime Thriller & Library Collection Opportunity

Dear [Librarian Name],

I hope this message finds you well! I'm a crime fiction author from [location], and I'm currently promoting my new thriller,

[Book Title]. I've been using your library system since [year], and it would be an honor to have my books available to your community of readers.

Synopsis: [Book Title] follows detective Emma Russo as she returns to her hometown of Ridgewood to settle her late father's estate—only to discover he was investigating a decades-old disappearance before his sudden death. When Emma begins asking questions, she uncovers a web of corruption involving the town's most powerful families, a pattern of silenced witnesses, and evidence that suggests her father's death was no accident. Racing against those who want the past buried, Emma must decide how far she'll go to expose the truth.

Comparative Titles: Fans of Tana French's *In the Woods* and William Kent Krueger's *Ordinary Grace* will recognize a shared DNA in [Book Title]—a small-town mystery where the past refuses to stay buried, family secrets run deep, and one determined investigator risks everything for justice.

I would love to collaborate with [Library Name] on an author talk, reading, or virtual Q&A, bringing this story directly to your patrons and creating a memorable experience for your community. I would be honored to donate a signed copy for evaluation and can provide promotional materials to support any programming.

For your convenience, I've attached my Author Media Kit with all the details you'll need, including ISBN, publisher, distribution details, and book synopsis.

Thank you so much for your time and consideration. I look forward to connecting!

With gratitude, [Your Name] [Your contact information] [Your website]

Your Author Media Kit

An Author Media Kit is your professional introduction in document form—part business card, part website, condensed into a single PDF that booksellers, librarians, and event coordinators can review in minutes. It contains every detail they need to make a decision about ordering your book or hosting an event, while also being visually compelling enough to make you stand out. Think of it as your book's resume: professional, comprehensive, and designed to open doors.

Contents:

- Author name and tagline
- Book title and subtitle (if applicable)
- Synopsis
- Series details (if applicable)
- Genre and target demographic
- Page count
- Comparable titles
- ISBN for all formats (Kindle, paperback, hardcover, audiobook)
- Release date
- Publisher name
- Distribution details (bookstores need to know where to order your book)
- Returns policy (some bookstores will only order your books if they're returnable)
- Available formats
- Keywords or themes
- Author bio and headshot
- Link to book trailer (if available)
- Editorial reviews, reader reviews, or testimonials

Format: Your Author Media Kit should be 2-4 pages in PDF format—easy to email and universally readable. Many authors use free design templates from platforms like Canva, which offers customizable media kit templates you can adapt with your own details. Keep it professional: your name and positioning statement at the top, clear sections for each element, and contact information where it's easy to find.

The Power of Showing Up

After sending your pitch email, wait about a week and then follow up. An in-person visit is a fantastic opportunity to put a face to a name, bring a physical copy of your book, make an impression, build rapport, and begin a new journey toward visibility and recognition in a new reading community.

This is where your ME Factor becomes lived experience. When you walk into that bookstore, you're not just another author asking for shelf space—you're a storyteller who believes in the power of your creative vision. You're someone who can articulate why your book matters, who it's for, and what it offers readers that nothing else does quite this way.

That confidence—the ability to stand in your work without apologizing—is something you build through practice. The first conversation might feel awkward. The fifth one will feel more natural. By the tenth, you'll find yourself genuinely enjoying these interactions, because you're talking about something you care about with people who love stories.

If a bookstore stocks your book, visit the store, thank them in person, and buy books from them. If they host an event for you, promote it enthusiastically, show up early, stay late, and send a handwritten thank-you note afterward. If a library adds your book to their collection, offer to do a free author talk for their patrons.

You'll invest time in these relationships because you're building genuine connections with people who will become part of your literary circle.

Example: A mystery author researched independent bookstores that regularly featured cozy mysteries. He sent personalized emails mentioning specific staff picks he'd noticed and offered to host a "mystery lover's coffee chat" where attendees could discuss their favorite mystery tropes. Three stores responded. One event led to the store adding his series to their standing mystery book club rotation.

Example: An author who wrote a health and wellness book targeted Barnes & Noble locations near yoga studios and wellness centers. She pitched a free workshop on "Creating Easy Self-Care Practices" timed to early January when many people initiate new wellness programs. Two stores agreed. She promoted the events to her email list and social media, drawing 35+ attendees. Both stores stocked her book, and the events resulted in local podcast interviews that amplified her visibility.

These examples represent what's possible when the timing, fit, book, and relationship align. Not every outreach will get a response, and many won't lead to events or partnerships. But each personalized pitch builds momentum, confidence, your network - results compound over time.

Offer value first, build relationships second. Sales may follow naturally.

Those relationships begin with how you make booksellers feel from first contact. You want booksellers to see you as memorable, and they want the same from you. Customize your pitch to show genuine familiarity with their store, and that reciprocity—making them feel valued and chosen—is what makes you unforgettable.

CALIBRATION: Recognizing Effective Outreach

Warning Signs:

❌ You're sending identical pitch emails to dozens of stores without personalization

❌ You're pitching events that only promote your book without serving the community

❌ You're not following up or showing gratitude after initial contact

Indicators of Success:

✔ Bookstores or libraries respond positively and express genuine interest in your work

✔ You're building repeat relationships—second books, follow-up events, referrals to other stores

✔ Your outreach leads to unexpected opportunities like media coverage, speaking invitations, or book club invitations

WORKROOM: Building Your Bookstore & Library Outreach Plan

LEVEL 1: ESSENTIAL (Start here) – 30 minutes

1. Identify 8-10 local bookstores in your home region that you've visited before—mix of independent stores and major chains
2. Research the name and email for the store manager, buyer, or community relations coordinator
3. Research 3-5 local library systems where you already have a library card (or get one now)
4. Identify the acquisitions librarian or programming coordinator at each library
5. Customize your pitch email using the examples in this chapter—personalize the synopsis, identify your audience segments, select comp titles, and add local, regional details
6. Create an Author Media Kit for the book you're pitching, save as PDF
7. Send your pitch emails with your Author Media Kit attached or linked

LEVEL 2: IF YOU WANT TO GO DEEPER

1. Expand your reach through bookstores and libraries outside of your home area
2. Attend events at these stores and libraries as a community member
3. Build relationships with booksellers and librarians in person and on social media
4. Offer to do joint events with other local authors

LEVEL 3: DEEP DIVE (Come back to this over weeks/months)

1. Create a spreadsheet tracking all contacts, correspondence dates, and outcomes

2. Develop multiple event concepts that serve different community interests
3. Build relationships with library consortiums and regional bookstore associations
4. Attend regional book festivals and trade shows where booksellers and librarians gather

This isn't about nationwide distribution. It's about building genuine relationships in your community that can amplify your visibility and create word-of-mouth momentum. It's about returning to the fundamental human act of storytelling—standing before another person and saying, "I have a story I think you'll care about."

In a world of algorithms and invisibility, these face-to-face connections ground us. We write because we feel compelled to create, to imagine things, to translate the world around us. The work itself is solitary and internal. But sharing that work—inviting others to learn about it, care about it, and read it—pulls us into our community.

Sometimes, the most powerful marketing you can do is to simply show up, hold your book in your hands, say "I wrote this," and see what happens next.

CHAPTER 16

BEYOND THE PAGE: YOUR VISIBILITY MULTIPLIERS

Your words live on pages, but your voice can reach readers in ways a book never will.

When someone hears you speak—on a podcast, book signing, radio interview, or on TikTok—something shifts. Your author headshot becomes three-dimensional. They hear your speaking voice, your personality, your humor, your empathy. They see your passion at work. That connection creates a level of trust and memorability that text alone can't replicate.

This chapter explores speaking engagements and media opportunities as extensions of your author brand and ME Factor—ways to amplify your authority, deepen reader connections, and build professional credibility that extends far beyond a single book.

WHAT: Multi-Dimensional Presence

Speaking engagements and media opportunities encompass a wide range of formats, each offering different ways to connect with audiences:

Speaking Gigs:

- Conference presentations and panels
- Workshops and training sessions
- Book signing events
- Library and bookstore author talks
- Book club appearances (virtual or in-person)
- Academic lectures or guest teaching
- Corporate speaking events for business book authors

Media Opportunities:

- Podcast, YouTube, radio interviews
- Newspaper articles or book reviews
- Magazine features or spreads
- Television appearances
- Online video series or web shows

Social Media Video Presence:

- TikTok/BookTok videos (including TikTok Live if you have 1,000+ followers)
- Instagram Reels
- YouTube content
- Facebook or LinkedIn Live sessions

- Stories and short-form video content

The common thread: all of these opportunities allow you to show up as a whole person, not just a name on a book cover. They transform your two-dimensional author brand into a living, breathing presence that readers can connect with on a deeper level.

WHY: The Strategic Value of Being Heard *and* Seen

Speaking and media opportunities offer many strategic advantages. When readers hear your voice or see you speak, you become real to them. Your book becomes a conversation. This human connection builds curiosity that transcends any single title you publish.

The Data: Podcast interviews provide long-term value, with 73% of Americans having listened to at least one podcast, and listeners spending an average of 6.3 hours per week with podcasts—creating sustained exposure that grows over time.

Building Authority and Credibility: Every speaking engagement or media appearance positions you as an expert— in your genre, your subject matter, or your area of expertise. For business book authors, this positions you as a thought leader whose ideas matter beyond your books. For fiction authors, it establishes you as someone who understands craft, genre, storytelling, and audience at a level worth listening to.

Your ME Factor in Action: Speaking and media appearances let you leverage your uniqueness to become a recurring, memorable presence for readers. Maybe it's your signature style—bold glasses, signature colors, recurring quips. These traits help readers remember you long after they've closed your book. "Oh, that's the author with the quill earrings," or "That's the one who starts every video with 'Here we go again!'" These details create familiarity, and familiarity builds trust.

Creating Unexpected Opportunities: Speaking and media exposure often lead to opportunities you couldn't predict. A podcast interview might lead to a consulting engagement. A conference presentation might result in a teaching invitation. A radio interview might connect you with another author for a collaboration. These ripple effects have the potential to extend your reach in ways that static marketing can't.

Deepening Reader Connection: Readers who hear you speak or see you in media develop a different relationship with your work. They feel like they know you. They're more likely to recommend your books, show up to future events, and become long-term fans—not just one-time buyers.

Networking and Community Building: Speaking events and media appearances connect you with other professionals in your field—authors, industry experts, thought leaders. These relationships can lead to referrals, collaborations, and ongoing support throughout your career.

Example: A romantic comedy author was invited to speak on a RomCom podcast about writing humor in contemporary romance. That podcast episode reached 40,000 listeners, many of whom had never heard of her. Three months later, she saw a spike in her backlist sales and received an invitation to speak at a romance fiction conference. One speaking engagement led to an opportunity at a writers' conference, which became an annual gig.

Example: An IT consultant published his second book and was invited to speak at a regional technology conference. His presentation impressed an attendee who worked in corporate training, leading to a six-month consulting contract. That contract generated more income than his book sales that year and resulted in speaking invitations at another company

The return isn't always immediate or linear, but visibility creates momentum. Every time you show up with your voice, personality, and expertise, you're building recognition and authority that serves your entire career.

HOW: Speaking With Purpose

Building a speaking and media presence doesn't require becoming a professional speaker or hiring a publicist. It starts with identifying opportunities aligned with your ME Factor and target readers, then approaching them strategically.

Claiming Your Power

If the idea of being seen and heard makes you uncomfortable, you're not alone—most writers prefer the cave and the laptop. But you don't necessarily need to be an extrovert or talk about everything—just to claim your expertise in 2-3 specific areas. These are your speaking pillars: the topics you intrinsically know and own, where your authority comes from lived experience, not performance. When you speak from this place, confidence isn't something you fake—it's something you already have.

Identifying the Right Opportunities

Not every speaking engagement or media opportunity serves

your goals. Use your ME Factor and reader personas (from Chapters 2 and 5) to evaluate whether an opportunity is worth your time and energy.

Ask yourself:

- Does this audience include my target readers?
- Does this align with my author brand and positioning?
- Will this reach people who care about my subject matter or genre?
- Does this feel authentic to who I am, or am I forcing something uncomfortable?

For business book authors, prioritize opportunities that position you as a thought leader in your field—industry conferences, business podcasts, professional development workshops.

For fiction authors, prioritize opportunities that connect you with readers who love your genre—genre-specific conferences, book clubs, reader-focused podcasts, bookstore events.

Pitching Yourself for Podcasts and Media

Most podcasts, radio shows, and media outlets are actively looking for guests. Your job is to make it easy for them to say yes.

Example podcast pitch:

Subject: Podcast Guest Pitch: AI, IT Strategy & Lessons from Enterprise Tech

Hello [Host Name],

I'm an IT consultant with 20+ years of corporate experience and a longtime listener of your podcast. I really value your collaborative interview style and the way you ground complex topics in practical, real-world insight.

I've recently published a new book, *Practical AI: Smarter IT Strategies for Leaders in a Rapidly Changing World*, and believe I'd be a strong fit for your audience—especially listeners interested in practical business innovation and responsible, scalable AI adoption beyond the hype.

I'd love to join you for a conversation about AI strategy, common enterprise IT pitfalls, and what leaders should be focusing on right now. My media kit is attached for reference.

Best regards, [Name]

For radio and traditional media: Local radio stations and newspapers are often open to featuring local authors. Do your research and tie your pitch request to a specific show and host, identifying how your book and your expertise will directly align with their current programming. Offer to tie your book to a timely topic or current event when possible.

For television or larger media outlets: These opportunities often require more established credentials or a publicist, but don't rule them out entirely. If your book addresses a trending topic or you have unique expertise, go for it. The worst they can say is no.

Preparing for Speaking Engagements

Preparation reduces anxiety and ensures you show up confidently:

Know your key messages: What 3-5 main points do you want the audience to remember? Write them down. Practice articulating them clearly and concisely.

Prepare stories and examples: People remember stories, not abstract concepts. Have 2-3 concrete examples or anecdotes ready that illustrate your key points.

Practice, but don't over-rehearse: You want to sound natural, not robotic. Practice enough to feel confident but leave room for spontaneity and authentic conversation.

Anticipate questions: Think about what your audience might ask and prepare thoughtful responses. For book signings or author talks, expect questions about your book, your writing process, inspiration, and advice for aspiring authors.

Test your tech: For virtual events, test your microphone, camera, lighting, and internet connection beforehand. Poor audio or video quality undermines your professionalism.

Look sharp and dress well: Don't overlook the confidence-value of *showing up well* and presenting yourself professionally. Why does this matter? To properly meet the moment, acknowledge your success, and reaffirm your authority. When you look polished and put-together, you feel more capable—and that confidence translates to energy and creative power.

Building Your Speaker/Media Kit

If you're pursuing multiple speaking opportunities, a Speaker/Media Kit can be helpful. However, if you don't have extensive speaking experience yet, your Author Media Kit (from Chapter 15) works perfectly fine for media pitches.

What to include in a Speaker Kit:

- Professional headshot
- Speaker bio (focusing on expertise and credentials)
- List of past speaking engagements with links or clips so the podcaster can hear your speaking style
- Your expertise topics
- Sample interview questions
- Contact information

Social Media Videos: Showing Up Authentically

Social media videos—TikTok, Instagram Reels, YouTube—offer a low-stakes way to practice showing up on camera and letting your personality shine through. If you're shy about being on camera, consider varying your content so that just 1 in every 10 posts is a video of you speaking. This gives your audience a chance to know you better.

Ideas for video content (keep all videos under 15 seconds to ensure people watch the whole thing):

- Quick book recommendations: "Hey Book Friends, here's a 10-second book recommendation..." (Best practice: sharing your video length up front)
- Behind-the-scenes of your writing process
- Answering reader questions
- Sharing a success and how you feel about it, or a failure and what you learned from it
- Reading a short excerpt from your book
- Talking about what inspired a particular scene or character

The goal isn't perfection—it's presence. Readers appreciate authenticity far more than polish. Let them see the real you.

The Art of Saying No

Here's the most important filter for deciding which opportunities to pursue: **Say no to things that don't feel good.**

If an invitation makes you think, "Oh God, do I have to?", it's okay to honor your preferences and capacity. Don't judge yourself. Saying no means you're saving your creative energy for something that genuinely excites you. Not every opportunity deserves your time, even if it seems prestigious or potentially beneficial. Your energy is finite. Spend it on opportunities that align with your goals.

Example: The RomCom author was invited to speak at a general writing conference three states away. The event didn't focus on her genre, travel would be challenging and expensive, and she just didn't want to go. She declined and instead chose a local book fair where she'd connect directly with readers who loved her work—and had way more fun doing it.

Example: The IT consultant was invited on a popular podcast with 100,000 listeners. The topic aligned perfectly with his book, and the audience matched his target demographic. Even though it required significant prep time, he was genuinely excited about the opportunity to show up as a thought leader. He said yes, and the exposure connected him with exactly the readers he'd been trying to reach: IT leaders seeking practical AI guidance.

The pattern: honor what feels good. Say yes when you're excited. Say no without guilt when you're not. Trust your instincts.

CALIBRATION: Recognizing Effective

Speaking and Media Presence

Warning Signs:

✖ You're accepting every speaking or media invitation out of fear of missing opportunities

✖ You're exhausted after events and resent the time and expense they require

✖ Opportunities aren't leading to any measurable outcomes (book sales, new connections, future invitations)

Indicators of Success:

✔ You're receiving unsolicited invitations based on past appearances

✔ Readers mention they discovered you through a specific podcast or event

✔ You feel more confident, more poised, more excited about new speaking opportunities because of recent speaking engagements

If you're seeing warning signs, reassess which opportunities you're saying yes to and why. Not every author needs to be a frequent speaker or media presence. Find the level that works for you.

WORKROOM: Building Your Speaking and Media Presence

LEVEL 1: ESSENTIAL (Start here) – 30 minutes

1. Identify 5-7 podcasts, radio shows, or media outlets that reach your target readers
2. Listen to several episodes to understand their audience and format
3. Draft a pitch email using the template in this chapter
4. Send pitches to 3-5 opportunities
5. Or record one 10-15 second video for social media introducing yourself and your book

LEVEL 2: IF YOU WANT TO GO DEEPER

1. Create a Speaker/Media Kit (or adapt your Author Media Kit for media use)
2. Research 3-5 local speaking opportunities (libraries, bookstores, community organizations) and reach out
3. Practice your key messages and stories until you can deliver them confidently
4. Record a 10-15 second video for social media discussing a topic related to your book

LEVEL 3: DEEP DIVE (Come back to this over weeks/months)

1. Develop 3-5 signature talk topics you can deliver at various events
2. Create a spreadsheet tracking all media and speaking opportunities, outcomes, and follow-up
3. Build relationships with podcast hosts and event organizers for repeat invitations
4. Establish a consistent video presence (monthly or quarterly) on social media

Your voice carries what your words alone cannot. Every time you step beyond the page—whether on a podcast, at a signing, or in a 10-second video—you're not just promoting a book.

You're bringing your unique positioning to life. You're showing readers the creator behind the prose, the passion behind the positioning, the authenticity behind your author brand.

You can do this. You're already doing it every time you talk about your book with a friend, explain your story to a stranger, or answer questions at an event. Are you willing to go a step further to deepen your impact? If that question excites you—even a little—you know you're on the right track.

CHAPTER 17

SELF-CARE: A COMPETITIVE ADVANTAGE

You've spent sixteen chapters learning how to build your ME Factor, position yourself strategically in the market, create visibility for your work, and engage with readers. Now let's talk about the one resource that makes all of it possible: YOU.

Real self-care isn't indulgent, and it's much more than bubble baths and candles. *Strategic* Self-Care is the foundation of career longevity. It's what allows you to write consistently, market authentically, show up for your readers, and sustain your author career for years—not just through a single book launch.

When you neglect yourself—your physical health, your emotional well-being, your creative energy—everything else suffers. Your writing quality declines. Your marketing feels forced. Your passion dims. But when you care for yourself regularly, you protect the very thing that makes your work possible: your capacity to create.

This chapter is about bringing strategy to that care, understanding what you need to be happy, and being real with yourself about the blockers that prevent it.

WHAT: Strategic Self-Care as Career Management

Strategic Self-Care goes deeper than typical wellness advice. It's a personal mastery and recalibration mindset made up of easy, actionable tactics that bring immediate value and support.

For authors, this approach addresses the unique challenges of a career that demands both creativity and business acumen, solitude and visibility, patience and hustle. You're asked to be vulnerable enough to create meaningful work, then confident enough to promote it publicly. You're asked to write for hours in isolation, then show up energized for in-person events. These contradictions create tension, and without intentional care, that tension can erode your well-being.

Strategic Self-Care is organized around five core practices:

Celebrating Small Wins: Acknowledging all successes, not just major milestones

Grieving Losses: Processing disappointment or rejection without letting it harden you

Saying No: Protecting your energy by being discerning about commitments

Practicing Imperfection: Releasing perfectionism that paralyzes creativity

Asking for Help: Recognizing you can't do everything alone

These five pillars are about being more intentional with what you're already doing. They're about alignment between what matters most and how you spend your time and energy.

WHY: The ROI of Creative Sustainability

Without this mindset, authors face creative paralysis, physical health issues, and career abandonment. The publishing industry doesn't talk much about author burnout, but it's pervasive. Authors who don't protect their energy, boundaries, and health eventually stop writing—not because they lose talent, but because they lose the capacity to sustain the work.

The Data: Neuroscience research published in 2024-2025 demonstrates that chronic stress significantly impairs both creativity and decision-making. For authors, this translates directly to career impact: difficulty writing or concentrating, poor strategic choices, and physical illness that prevents you from meeting deadlines or showing up for events.

But here's the flip side: authors who prioritize stress management report higher productivity, better work quality, and longer career trajectories. When you're physically healthy, emotionally balanced, and energetically aligned with your work, you write better books. You market with more authenticity. You show up for readers with genuine enthusiasm rather than performative energy.

This creates a competitive advantage because creative sustainability is rare. Many authors sprint through their first book launch, then disappear—exhausted, discouraged, or burned out. Authors who build long-term careers aren't necessarily the most talented—they're the ones who learn how to sustain their energy, protect their boundaries, and care for themselves as an ongoing practice.

Example: A fantasy author published three novels in three years, maintaining a relentless marketing schedule while working a full-time job. By year four, he was physically exhausted and creatively depleted. He couldn't write, he resented marketing and considered quitting entirely. After stepping back to implement these practices—regular rest, saying no to non-essential commitments, celebrating small wins—he gradually rebuilt his relationship with writing. It took nearly two years before he felt ready to publish again, but when he did, he approached it differently: slower marketing cadence, clearer boundaries, and genuine enjoyment of the process rather than forcing himself through it.

The return on investment for this approach isn't measured in a single quarter or book launch. It's measured in years—in your ability to still be writing, still be excited about your work, still be showing up for readers a decade from now.

HOW: The Five Pillars in Practice

Strategic Self-Care begins with awareness—noticing where you're depleting yourself and identifying small, actionable changes that restore your energy. Here's how to implement the five pillars:

Celebrating Small Wins

It's easy to celebrate big wins—a book deal, a bestseller list, a major award. Those are obvious, but they don't come often. Without feeding yourself a steady diet of self-acceptance and daily encouragement, you can grow cold inside, lose motivation, and emotionally check out.

A small win could be finishing a difficult chapter, receiving a thoughtful reader email, or posting on social media without anxiety. How do you celebrate it? If you've received praise, print out the email and tape it to your workspace so you see it several times a day. This visually reinforces your success, building self-appreciation and confidence. Or buy yourself a small gift. Every time you see it, you'll be reminded of the win, and that success will help you attract more successes.

Stop waiting for permission to acknowledge your progress. You don't need external validation. If you showed up, did the work, and moved your career forward, that's worth celebrating.

Grieving Losses

Authors face constant rejection—agents who pass, reviews that sting, events that flop, sales that disappoint. The instinct is either to pretend it doesn't hurt or to let it consume you. Neither works. What does work is processing disappointment quickly so it doesn't derail you.

Here's the practice: When something stings, give yourself five minutes. Sit with it. Acknowledge what hurts and why. Then ask: "Is there one constructive thing I can learn from this?" Sometimes the answer is yes—a better pitch, a clearer positioning, a different venue. Sometimes the answer is no—it just wasn't the right fit.

Either way, the practice is the same: feel it, learn what you can, then release it. This isn't about becoming numb. It's about building resilience so rejection doesn't derail you. The more you practice this, the less power any single rejection has to derail your momentum.

Saying No

Saying no disappoints people—there's no way around it. But saying yes when you mean no depletes you faster than any deadline or marketing campaign ever could. Every misaligned yes drains energy you need for your actual work.

Start small: decline a book club appearance during your writing time, skip a draining networking event, say no to beta-reading when you're on deadline. Practice with lower-stakes situations first, and you'll build the confidence to protect what matters most—your creative energy.

Practicing Imperfection

Perfectionism paralyzes creativity. It's often rooted in the fear that you won't be valued if you're not flawless—but that fear can prevent you from finishing and sharing your work.

Practice imperfection deliberately: post a social media video without perfect lighting, speak at an event without having every answer rehearsed, launch your website before the design feels completely finished, or pitch yourself for opportunities before you feel "ready." Start small. Notice that your world doesn't end, your readers don't abandon you, and you've reclaimed creative freedom. Your readers don't need you to be perfect— they need you to show up authentically so they have the opportunity to know you.

Asking for Help

Ego, pride, and past disappointments can keep you from asking for help—but pushing yourself beyond reasonable limits to avoid asking is just another form of avoidance. You can't sustain your career by holding everything up alone.

For authors, this might mean hiring help for admin tasks, asking a fellow author to beta-read, delegating social media during heavy writing periods, or requesting a deadline extension when you're overwhelmed. Asking for help isn't weakness—it's recognition that sustainable creativity requires knowing when to share the load.

Physical Health and Workspace Essentials

Beyond emotional and psychological self-care, physical health directly impacts your ability to sustain your writing career. Consider these essentials:

Movement: Escaping your writing desk to walk, stretch, or exercise supports cognitive function and creativity. A 10-minute walk can reset your mind and unlock solutions to plot problems.

Hydration: Staying hydrated sharpens concentration and decision-making. Keep water at your desk.

Rest: Quality sleep fuels better writing and makes challenges feel manageable instead of overwhelming.

Ergonomics: A comfortable workspace supports sustained focus. A quality desk chair, proper lighting, and monitor positioning at the right height protect your body and make writing sessions more enjoyable.

Nutrition: Real food that sustains energy throughout the day supports mental clarity and creative stamina.

These physical foundations support career longevity. When you care for your body, you protect your capacity to create work that matters for years to come.

Checking In with Your WHY

Your WHY—your reason for writing, your deeper purpose—isn't static. It evolves as you grow, as your life circumstances change, as you gain experience in the industry.

Strategic Self-Care includes regularly checking in with yourself: Has your WHY changed in the past year? Are you still enjoying this path? If your activities don't match your underlying purpose, that disconnect can drain your energy and passion.

Ask yourself:

- Am I still excited about this work?
- What parts of my author career bring me joy?
- What parts drain me?
- If I could change one thing to enjoy this more, what would it be?

These questions help you recalibrate before misalignment becomes a bigger problem. The answer might be small adjustments or significant pivots—but you can't course-correct without pausing to assess where you are.

Self-Appreciation and What You Choose to Notice

The inner critic is relentless: you're not doing enough, other authors are further ahead, you should be everywhere at once. That voice will always exist. But you can choose not to give it power.

Self-appreciation is a practice. It means actively noticing what you've accomplished, what you're learning, the impact you're making—even if it's small. It means choosing to direct your attention toward what's working rather than constantly cataloging what's missing.

This isn't about pretending everything is perfect. It's about recognizing that where you focus your attention shapes your experience—and your capacity to keep going.

CALIBRATION: Burnout vs. Intentional Well Being

Warning Signs of Burnout:

❌ **You resent writing or marketing tasks that used to excite you**

❌ **You're constantly exhausted despite adequate sleep**

❌ **You're saying yes to everything out of guilt or obligation, not genuine desire**

Indicators of Success:

✔ **You feel energized (not drained) after writing sessions**

✓ **You're able to say no to opportunities that don't align with your goals without guilt**

✓ **You're celebrating progress and feeling genuine pride in what you're accomplishing**

If you're seeing warning signs, it's your system telling you something needs to adjust – and an opportunity to listen and re-evaluate.

WORKROOM: Building Your Strategic Self-Care Practice

LEVEL 1: ESSENTIAL (Start here) – 30 minutes

1. **Check in with your WHY**: Write one paragraph about why you write. Has this changed in the past year? Does your current work align with this rationale?
2. **Assess physical needs**: Identify one physical need you're neglecting and commit to addressing it this week.
3. **Evaluate your workspace**: Is your desk ergonomically sound? Do you have adequate lighting? Is your chair comfortable for multi-hour writing sessions? Make one improvement to your workspace.
4. **Celebrate one small win**: Identify something you accomplished this month (no matter how small) and celebrate it in a tangible way.
5. **Practice one NO**: Identify one request or obligation you can decline this week to protect your energy and strengthen your boundaries.

LEVEL 2: IF YOU WANT TO GO DEEPER

1. **Implement the 5 Pillars**: Choose one pillar

(celebrating small wins, grieving losses, saying no, practicing imperfection, asking for help) and practice it intentionally for 30 days.

2. **Audit your commitments**: List everything you've said yes to in the past three months. Which align with your goals? Which drain you? Identify 2-3 commitments you can release or renegotiate.

3. **Build a routine**: Design a weekly schedule that includes dedicated writing time, rest, movement, and social connection. Test it for one month and adjust based on what works.

LEVEL 3: DEEP DIVE (Come back to this over weeks/months)

1. **Quarterly self-care review**: Every 90 days, assess your energy levels, creative output, and overall satisfaction with your author career. What's working? What needs adjustment?

2. **Create a burnout prevention plan**: Identify your personal warning signs of burnout and create specific strategies to address them before they become critical.

3. **Build your support system**: Identify 2-3 people (fellow authors, family members, a coach or mentor) who can support you when you're struggling. Ask them explicitly if they're willing to be part of your support system.

Strategic Self-Care isn't a detour from building your author career—it's part of the foundation. The authors who sustain long-term success aren't the ones who work the hardest or sacrifice the most. They're the ones who protect their energy, honor their boundaries, and care for themselves with the same intention they bring to their writing and marketing.

Celebrate what you're accomplishing. Be discerning about what you take on. Give yourself permission to be human, to rest, to say no, to be more comfortable with imperfection.

Sometimes, the most strategic thing you can do is take care of yourself and trust that consistent energy and intention will carry you forward.

PART VII

LONGEVITY: THE 90-DAY RHYTHM

Strategic careers require ongoing assessment and adjustment. This is about using efficiency and intelligence to build repeatable processes, not just launching books.

In this section, debut authors will establish a career management system from the start—giving you a framework for ongoing assessment and strategic decision-making as your career evolves.

Published authors will create the pause you need to assess what's working, diagnose what's not, and make strategic adjustments before investing another year in tactics that don't serve you.

Returning authors will establish a quarterly rhythm that keeps you aligned with your goals, your energy, and the evolving market—without constant hustle.

CHAPTER 18

STAY SHARP, STAY STRATEGIC

You've spent years building your presence—shaping how you show up in the literary world, refining what makes you memorable, creating a platform that reflects who you are.

Now the essential question: Is it working?

Not "Should I be doing more?" but "Is what I'm doing moving me toward the author career I want—and does it still feel like me?"

That's what a quarterly review reveals. It's not a report card or a performance evaluation. It's a structured pause where you step back, assess what's changed, and decide whether those changes are serving you—or whether it's time to adjust.

The 90-day cycle isn't arbitrary. It's long enough for new habits to take root, for patterns to emerge, for you to see whether the effort you've invested is creating the outcomes you wanted. And it's short enough that if something's not working, you can catch it before you've burned six months or a year on the wrong path.

Change is inevitable. The tools or platforms you thought would work might not. Quarterly assessment gives you permission to notice—and adjust accordingly.

This is where reflection becomes strategy. Where effort becomes insight. Where you stop reacting and start directing your own evolution.

WHAT: Assessment as the Foundation of Career Growth

A structured pause—a moment to step off the treadmill of writing, editing, and promotion to ask yourself: *What's different? What's working? What needs to change?*

This isn't about vanity metrics or follower counts. It's about assessing the health and direction of your author career. Ask yourself the following questions:

- **Platform coherence:** Do your social media channels, website, newsletter, and Amazon presence align and reinforce the same message?
- **Engagement depth:** Are you building meaningful connections with readers, or creating surface-level interactions that never convert to loyalty?
- **Energy and sustainability:** Does your current approach feel manageable, or are you burning energy

on activities that deliver diminishing returns?
- **Directional alignment:** Are the changes you've implemented in the past 90 days moving you closer to your goals?

This isn't about judging yourself. It's about gathering honest intelligence—what's creating momentum, what's creating friction—then using that insight to make informed decisions about where to invest your finite time and energy next.

WHY: Reflection Reveals What Execution Cannot

You can work extraordinarily hard and still end up exhausted, off-course, or building the wrong things if you never pause to assess effort against outcomes.

The Data: Publishers report that regularly auditing book metadata and author platform elements is one of the most effective ways to improve visibility and long-term book sales revenue. In fact, books with complete and optimized metadata experience up to a 75% increase in sales, and authors who routinely audit and update their metadata see ongoing increases in discoverability. Structured reflection isn't additional work—it's the mechanism that ensures your work is effective.

Without regular assessment, you risk continuation bias: maintaining what you've always done simply because you've always done it, not because it still serves you. You accept opportunities that drained you last quarter because you fear losing momentum. You sustain social media accounts that generate no meaningful engagement because abandoning them feels like failure.

A structured pause interrupts that pattern and asks: *If I were starting fresh today, knowing what I know now, would I still make these same choices?*

For business executives: You already understand the value of quarterly business reviews—assessing KPIs, budget allocation, team performance, strategic alignment. This is that same discipline applied to your author platform. You're measuring what matters, not just what's easy to count.

For creative authors: You already know the power of stepping back from your manuscript to see it clearly. You finish a draft, create distance, then return with fresh perspective to identify what's working and what needs revision. This applies that same commitment to your career. You're not abandoning your vision—you're refining your approach.

Effort without assessment becomes exhausting guesswork. You pour energy into tactics without knowing if they're creating the outcomes you want. Regular reflection transforms effort into intelligence—and intelligence into strategic advantage.

Recommendation: As part of your assessment, step completely away from your author work for one full week. No writing. No editing. No marketing. No social media. Give yourself genuine distance. You cannot assess something clearly when you're still immersed in it. Engage with different activities. Let your mind rest and recalibrate. You'll return with clarity you couldn't access while executing.

HOW: Conducting Your Assessment

This isn't a massive audit. It's a focused conversation with yourself, organized around five core questions. Block out about an hour—and the clarity you gain will prevent months of misdirected effort.

1. Revisit Your ME Factor

Return to Chapter 2 and reread the ME Factor you defined: *Goal + Audience + YOU = Your Positioning.*

Ask yourself:

- Does this still feel accurate?
- Has anything shifted in how I think about my goal, my audience, or what makes me uniquely *me*?
- Am I bringing more of my authentic self into my outreach, marketing, and reader interactions than I was 90 days ago? Where can I see evidence of this?

You're not looking for complete reinvention – just subtle evolution. Places where you've gained clarity, changed priorities, or discovered new language that better captures who you are. Maybe your goal remains constant, but your understanding of your audience has sharpened. Maybe *you* haven't changed, but you've found more confident ways to express what makes you different.

Document what's evolved. Even small shifts create noticeable clarity over time.

2. Assess Behavioral Change

Reflect on the past 90 days. What are you doing differently now?

This isn't about measuring output. It's about noticing evolution:

- Have you established more consistent rhythms on platforms you enjoy using?
- Did you start declining opportunities that don't align with your brand—freeing energy for better ones?
- Have you leaned into content pillars that generate stronger reader response than you anticipated?
- Do your interactions with readers feel more natural, more reciprocal, more like genuine conversation?

Behavioral change reveals alignment. When you start showing up in ways that feel authentically *you*, readers respond—because authenticity is magnetic.

3. Evaluate Platform Performance and Engagement

Examine your platforms—social media, website, newsletter, Amazon presence—and assess which platforms are delivering the most value:

- **Where is engagement deepening?** Not just likes and follows, but comments, shares, direct messages, meaningful conversations?
- **What content resonates most strongly?** Are certain topics, formats, or content pillars generating disproportionate response?
- **Is your platform alignment tightening?** Do your profile picture, positioning statement, and brand message feel more consistent across channels than they did 90 days ago?
- **What platforms feel sustainable?** Which ones energize you, and which drain you without delivering proportional return?

A memoir author might realize: "My newsletter open rates have climbed from 22% to 41% since I started sharing more vulnerable, personal stories. Meanwhile, creating Instagram stories is labor-intensive and generates almost no response. I'm shifting my energy entirely to email."

An IT consultant writing about workplace technology might realize: "Speaking at industry conferences is where I come alive—attendees buy my book afterward, and several have become consulting clients. Twitter requires constant effort for minimal return. I'm investing in more speaking opportunities and letting Twitter go."

You're looking for two specific indicators:

- **What's delivering results?**
- **What can you sustain long-term?**

The goal isn't to be everywhere doing everything. It's to do what works *for you.*

4. Check Your Energy and Alignment

This question is deceptively simple but critically important: Are you more energized or more depleted than you were 90 days ago?

If you're implementing strategies from this book and feeling *more* exhausted, something is misaligned. Strategy should focus your energy, not scatter it.

Ask yourself:

- What specific activities are energizing me right now?
- What's depleting me?
- Am I saying no to opportunities that don't serve my goals?

- Am I celebrating progress, or only focused on what's still incomplete?

If your assessment reveals burnout, you now have the information you need to recalibrate. That awareness is invaluable.

5. Assess Direction and Trajectory

Step back and look at the larger picture: Are the changes you've made over the past 90 days moving you toward the author career you want?

Not the career you think you're *supposed* to want. Not the one that looks successful from the outside. The one that feels aligned with who you are and how you want to spend your finite creative energy.

Ask yourself:

- Am I building a platform that feels like an authentic extension of my work?
- Are the readers I'm attracting the ones I genuinely want to connect with?
- Is my approach maintainable long term, or am I doing something I'll eventually abandon?
- What would I change if I could start fresh today?

That last question is key. If, knowing what you know now, you'd make different choices, you have permission to make those changes. Nothing about your current approach is permanent. This pause gives you structured permission to evolve.

CALIBRATION: Effective Assessments

Warning Signs:

✗ You're completing the review out of obligation, not gaining actual insight

✗ You're noticing the same problems quarter after quarter without making changes

✗ The assessment reveals exhaustion and misalignment—but you're not taking action

Indicators of Success:

✔ You're noticing specific behavioral changes and can articulate why they happened

✔ Each quarter reveals clearer understanding of your ME Factor and what works for you

✔ The assessment leads to concrete adjustments that improve alignment and energy

If you're seeing warning signs, the review itself isn't the problem—that awareness is the first step toward meaningful change.

WORKROOM: Your Quarterly Review Process

LEVEL 1: ESSENTIAL (Start here) – 30 minutes

Schedule this every 90 days. Work through the 5 assessment

questions in the HOW section above. Don't overthink—this is a quick first pass to spot what needs attention. Document your key insights and identify ONE adjustment for next quarter.

LEVEL 2: IF YOU WANT TO GO DEEPER (Optional - 90 minutes)

If you want a more comprehensive assessment, expand your reflection:

Step 1: Review your SWOT analysis from Chapter 10. What's shifted? Have new opportunities emerged? Have previous threats diminished or intensified?

Step 2: Assess your content pillars from Chapter 8. Are you using them consistently? Do they still feel true to your brand, or has your focus evolved?

Step 3: Evaluate your platform alignment from Chapter 11. Are your profile picture, positioning statement, and visual/verbal brand consistent across all channels? What needs updating?

Step 4: Review your reader personas from Chapter 5. Are you creating content that speaks directly to them? Are they showing up where you expected? Have you learned anything new about them this quarter?

Step 5: Identify 2-3 specific adjustments you'll implement over the next quarter based on what you've learned.

LEVEL 3: DEEP DIVE (Come back to this over weeks and months)

For those who want to build quarterly assessment into a long-term career development practice:

Step 1: Create a simple tracking document where you record each assessment. Include:

- Date
- Key behavioral changes noticed
- Energy assessment (What's energizing me? What's depleting me?)
- One thing I'm celebrating this quarter
- One adjustment I'm implementing next quarter

Step 2: Once you have 3-4 documented assessments, look for patterns. Are you consistently energized by the same activities? Consistently drained by others? Those patterns are strategic intelligence about how you work best.

There's no right way to interpret results—what matters is that you're noticing patterns, honoring what they reveal about you, and using that insight to make aligned decisions.

Step 3: Use those patterns to inform bigger strategic decisions: Which platforms should you abandon entirely? Which opportunities deserve more investment? Where should you focus your energy to create the greatest return—not just financially, but in terms of fulfillment and career satisfaction?

Step 4: Share your process with an accountability partner—another author, a critique partner, or trusted colleague. Schedule conversations where you discuss what's changed, what's working, and what needs adjustment. Narrating your observations aloud often reveals deeper insights.

This transforms assessment into long-term career development discipline. You're not just evaluating the last 90 days—you're building a body of knowledge and self-awareness that will serve you for years to come.

Reflection without judgment. Evolution without abandonment. Growth without losing yourself.

Every 90 days, you have the chance to ask: *Am I still aligned with what matters to me? Am I building something real, something I care about? Am I showing up authentically?*

You don't need perfect answers. You just need the courage to keep asking honest questions—and the wisdom to adjust when something's not working.

The tools in this book give you strategy, clarity, and direction. But this pause—this intentional moment of reflection—is where those tools become a practice. Where discipline becomes wisdom. Where you stop performing and start evolving with intention.

Your presence in the literary world isn't static. Neither are you. The quarterly review honors that evolution—and gives you permission to level-up into the next version of you...and shine.

CONCLUSION

DIFFERENTIATION AS A DISCIPLINE

You opened this book facing a market of four million new titles competing for attention every year.

You knew your work deserved to be seen. You just weren't sure how to make that happen in a landscape this crowded and overwhelming.

Visibility is clarity - about who you are, where you fit, who you serve, and the promise you make to readers that only you can keep.

You've done the work now. You've defined your ME Factor. You've identified your emotional promise. You've studied your market, built your reader personas, and positioned yourself strategically in spaces where your readers are actively searching. You've synthesized all of that into an author brand that's recognizable, memorable, and unmistakably yours.

But here's what matters most: **You've given yourself permission to show up authentically.**

Not the author you think you should be. Not a manufactured persona designed to chase trends. Not a watered-down version of your authentic voice shaped by what you think the market wants.

You.

Your perspective. Your expertise. Your voice. Your emotional signature. The specific combination of elements that makes your work yours—and no one else's.

That permission—that willingness to stand in your ME Factor and say "this is who I am, this is what I offer, I honor it, and it matters"—is the most powerful marketing decision you will ever make.

What You've Built

You've claimed your identity. In Part I, you discovered your ME Factor—the intersection of your goal, your audience, and what makes you uniquely you—and defined the emotional promise readers can count on from your work.

You've gathered intelligence. In Part II, you identified your competitive set, built detailed reader personas, and found the white space where your authentic work meets genuine reader demand.

You've synthesized a brand. In Part III, you defined your content pillars and created brand consistency that connects everything you write—regardless of genre, topic, or format.

You've assessed your position. In Part IV, you conducted a SWOT analysis and platform audit that gave you strategic perspective most authors lack.

You've built digital visibility. In Part V, you created content strategies that align all your platforms so they amplify each other instead of scattering your impact.

You've embraced human connection. In Part VI, you learned to pitch bookstores and libraries, explore speaking opportunities, and stand in your work without apologizing for it.

You've protected your creative energy. In Part VII, you recognized that strategic self-care is the foundation of career longevity and built a 90-day review cycle to keep you aligned with what matters.

That's active strategy-building.

And now you have something rare: a strategic foundation created with intention and purpose.

Differentiation as Ongoing Practice

Here's the truth about differentiation: it's not something you achieve once and maintain passively.

Markets shift. Reader appetites evolve. New authors enter your space. Platforms change their algorithms. Your own work grows and changes as you gain experience and confidence.

Differentiation isn't a destination. It's an ongoing discipline of noticing what's changed, assessing whether your positioning still serves you, and adjusting with intention rather than reacting with panic.

Every 90 days, you'll pause and ask: *Am I still aligned? Am I still myself? Am I building the career I want?*

Some quarters, the answer will be yes—keep going. Other quarters, you'll notice misalignments that need adjustment. Maybe a platform that once worked has stopped serving you. Maybe your reader personas have evolved. Or maybe your ME Factor has sharpened as you've gained clarity about what makes you different…and maybe that makes you want *more*, giving you the confidence to try something new.

Those adjustments are signs that you're paying attention, staying strategic, and refusing to let momentum carry you in a direction that no longer fits.

The authors who build successful careers aren't the ones who nail everything perfectly the first time. They're the ones who experiment, who assess regularly, adjust intentionally, and trust themselves enough to pivot when something's not working.

You now have the frameworks to do that. Every tool in this book is designed to be revisited, refined, and evolved as your career grows.

What to Carry Forward

As you close this book and return to the work of writing,

editing, and marketing, these are the truths worth remembering:

1. Your ME Factor is your north star. Goal + Audience + YOU = Your positioning. When you're confused about what to do next, return to this formula. Does this decision serve your goal? Does it reach your audience? Does it feel like you? If yes to all three, move forward.

2. It's okay to do less. You don't need to be on every platform or pursue every opportunity. Success isn't about exhausting yourself—it's about understanding what works for you and being discerning about where you invest your energy.

3. Saying no protects your yes. Every time you decline something that doesn't serve your positioning, you're protecting energy for something that does. Celebrate the discernment that lets you recognize what's worth your time.

4. Consistency compounds over time. Every aligned action builds on the one before it. Your second book launch is easier than your first. Your hundredth social media post benefits from the ninety-nine that came before. Trust the process of showing up consistently as yourself.

5. You have everything you need. The frameworks. The tools. The strategic clarity. And most importantly—the courage to show up as yourself in a crowded market. That courage is rare. Honor it.

One Final Truth

Stories hold the world together. They help us make sense of our experiences, connect with each other, and preserve what matters. Your stories—whether fiction or nonfiction—are part of that essential tradition.

The work you do matters. Not just to you, but to the readers who will find themselves in your pages, who will discover solutions in your frameworks, who will feel less alone because you wrote honestly about something true.

But those readers can't be moved by your work if they never discover it. That's why visibility matters. Not because marketing is the point of writing—but because marketing is how your writing finds the people who need it most.

You've defined your ME Factor. You've built your strategic foundation. You've given yourself permission to show up authentically in the literary world.

Your job as a writer is to be visible and memorable.

Now go stand in that positioning with confidence. Trust that the readers who need your work will find it—because you've made yourself recognizable and unmistakably you. Your story deserves to be heard, and now you know it will be.

GLOSSARY

A+ Content (Amazon) - Enhanced product page features with rich graphics and formatted text (Chapter 14)

Algorithm - System that determines content visibility and recommendations on platforms (Chapters 12, 13, 14)

Amazon Author Central - Author profile management platform for Amazon book pages (Chapter 14)

Amazon KDP (Kindle Direct Publishing) - Amazon's self-publishing platform for ebooks and print books (Chapter 14)

Analytics - Data tracking tools that measure platform and content performance (Chapter 11)

Backlist - Previously published books in an author's catalog (Chapter 6)

Brand Consistency - Maintaining recognizable visual and verbal identity across all platforms (Chapters 9, 11)

Brand Filter - Three questions to evaluate whether opportunities align with your positioning (Chapter 7)

Brand Through-Line - The consistent emotional experience readers expect from all your work (Chapter 7)

Call to Action (CTA) - Invitation for readers to take a specific next step (Conclusion)

Comp Titles (Comparable Titles) - Books similar to yours used to understand positioning and market (Chapter 4)

Competitive Benchmarking - Identifying what differentiates you from similar authors (Chapter 4)

Content Pillars - The 3-5 core themes organizing all your public-facing content (Chapter 8)

Conversion / Conversion Rate - When someone takes a desired action in response to your marketing. Soft conversions are email signups, social follows, link clicks. Hard conversions are purchases. Conversion rate measures the percentage of viewers who take action. (Chapters 5, 11, 14)

Discoverability - How easily readers can find your book through search and browsing (Chapters 6, 14)

Emotional Promise - The consistent feeling readers experience from your work (Chapter 3)

Engagement Rate - Measure of meaningful interaction versus passive viewing (Chapters 11, 13)

Genre - Category of literature with specific conventions and reader expectations (Chapter 2)

HEA (Happily Ever After) - Romance genre term for the guaranteed happy/satisfying romantic resolution readers expect (Chapter 6, 11)

ISBN - International Standard Book Number, unique identifier for books (Chapter 15)

Keywords - Words and phrases readers type into search engines when looking for books. Examples: "cozy mystery bookstore," "burnout prevention strategies." Match reader language, not industry jargon. (Chapters 4, 9, 14)

Market Gaps - Underserved reader needs where demand exceeds supply (Chapter 6)

Market Intelligence - Understanding competitive landscape, reader behavior, and opportunities (Chapter 4)

ME Factor - Your unique positioning formula: Goal + Audience + YOU (Chapter 2)

Metadata - Data describing your book (keywords, categories, description) that aids discovery (Chapter 14)

Metrics - Measurable data points tracking performance and engagement (Chapter 11)

Open Rate (Email) - Percentage of newsletter recipients who open your email (Chapter 11)

Persona (Reader Persona) - Detailed profile of your ideal reader based on observed patterns (Chapter 5)

Positioning - How you distinctively place yourself in the market relative to competitors (Chapters 2, 6)

Reader Personas (Primary and Secondary) - The 2-3 detailed profiles of readers most likely to love your work (Chapter 5)

ROI (Return on Investment) - Value gained relative to time, money, or energy invested (Chapter 10)

SEO (Search Engine Optimization) - Using strategic keywords in your website and content to help search engines connect your work to readers searching for books like yours. (Chapters 4, 9)

Self-Publishing - Publishing your book independently without a traditional publisher (Chapter 14)

Social Proof - Evidence that others value your work (reviews, testimonials, endorsements) (Chapter 14)

Strategic Self-Care - The 5 Pillars framework for enduring author career management (Chapter 17)

Subgenre - Specialized category within a larger genre (Chapter 6)

SWOT Analysis - Assessment of Strengths, Weaknesses, Opportunities, and Threats (Chapter 10)

Target Audience - The specific readers your work is intended to reach and serve (Chapter 5)

White Space - Market opportunity where your authentic work meets unmet reader demand (Chapter 6)

ABOUT THE AUTHOR

Lisa Towles bridges two worlds that rarely intersect: high-level business strategy and the lived experience of being a working author. With an MBA in IT Management and 18 years in corporate communications, she built her career translating complex business objectives into market differentiation and revenue results. She holds multiple certifications in digital marketing and AI implementation and has served as Board President of an award-winning nonprofit, leading strategic planning and mission-driven growth at the organizational level.

Lisa is also an award-winning crime novelist with 14 published books spanning 20 years. As an active member of Mystery Writers of America, Sisters in Crime, and International Thriller Writers, she's navigated every corner of the publishing industry —small presses, academic publishers, hybrid models, traditional deals, and self-publishing—learning what drives author visibility and sustainable author careers. Her most recent thriller, *Switch,* was published in 2025 and won a Readers' Choice Book Award.

For 16 years, Lisa has mentored writers on author platform building, book marketing strategy, and strategic positioning in crowded markets. In 2024, she formalized this work as Story Impact Consulting, bringing her dual expertise to help authors discover their competitive advantage: authentic author branding that honors who they are rather than forcing them to be someone they're not.

Her work centers on one core belief: in author marketing, YOU are your own secret weapon.

Learn more about Lisa at lisatowles.com or connect with her on LinkedIn.

ACKNOWLEDGEMENTS

Writing a book that bridges business strategy and creative practice requires standing in both worlds simultaneously—and I couldn't have done that alone.

This is my second nonfiction book and my first since the early 1990s, after which came fifteen crime thrillers. Those two decades of fiction writing taught me storytelling. My eighteen years in corporate communications and marketing taught me strategy. But it took twenty years navigating the publishing landscape—through small victories and plenty of failures—to understand what actually moves the needle for author careers. This book exists because of everyone who helped me translate that hard-won knowledge into a framework others can use.

To my publishing team: Lisa Orban, thank you for your leadership, expertise, patience, and vision. You made this book better at every stage.

To my editors: Cindy Davis and Ana Manwaring—I've learned so much from your precision, insight, and commitment to clarity. You pushed me to sharpen every framework until it was genuinely useful.

To Nikki Davenport: Thank you for your deep awareness and smart guidance. Your perspective strengthened this work in ways I couldn't have achieved alone.

To friend and fellow author Ed DeJesus: You provided the final nudge to finish this book when I needed it most. Thank you for believing it mattered.

To my husband, Lee: You model authenticity so beautifully, every single day. Watching you show up as yourself—without apology, without performance—inspires me to reach for my own ME Factor. Thank you for making that look possible.

To my family: Thank you for always making time to read my work, edit my drafts, and reassure and encourage me. Your love and support is the backbone of my creativity.

And to every author who's ever felt invisible in a crowded market, who's worked hard without seeing results, who's wondered if their voice matters—this book is for you. Your stories deserve to be heard. I hope these frameworks help you make that happen.

AUTHOR SUPPORT

The frameworks in this book have been tested with hundreds of authors across every career stage and publishing path. Some implement them independently with remarkable success. Others have found that having a strategic partner—someone who's navigated both the creative and business sides of publishing for two decades—accelerates their timeline and sharpens their positioning in ways they couldn't achieve alone.

Writing is solitary work. You spend months—sometimes years—alone with your manuscript, developing characters, refining arguments, perfecting prose. But then comes the shift: suddenly you're expected to be a strategist, a marketer, a brand manager, a content creator. You're defining your ME Factor, conducting SWOT analyses, building reader personas, optimizing metadata, creating content pillars, and showing up on platforms where you're supposed to be both authentic and strategic.

It's a lot. And you're doing it alone.

Many authors find that the hardest part isn't learning the frameworks—it's applying them to their own work with objectivity. When you're deep in your own career, it's difficult to see patterns you might be missing. You second-guess your positioning. You wonder if your emotional promise is clear enough. You struggle to articulate what makes you different when you're too close to your own work to see it.

That's where strategic partnership creates value—not because you can't do this work, but because having an experienced perspective accelerates clarity. Someone who can spot the patterns in your reader reviews that reveal your actual audience. Someone who can help you see the competitive advantages you're too modest to claim. Someone who recognizes when your brand expression has drifted across platforms and knows how to realign it.

Strategic Self-Care becomes easier when you're not carrying the weight alone. The discipline of quarterly reviews feels less daunting when someone's there to help you interpret what you're seeing. Saying no to opportunities that don't serve your positioning becomes clearer when you have a strategic filter you trust. The vulnerability of showing up authentically in your marketing feels less risky when you have support that reminds you why your authentic voice is your competitive advantage.

Story Impact Consulting works with authors who value strategic clarity and want to build successful, differentiated author careers. The approach combines business strategy frameworks with deep understanding of the creative process—recognizing that authors aren't products to be marketed, but professionals building long-term career assets.

Strategic support takes many forms—from comprehensive career positioning to targeted guidance on specific challenges —with every engagement calibrated to deliver measurable outcomes aligned with your current reality and future vision. Whether you need accountability to conduct your SWOT analysis, directional guidance on which platforms deserve your energy, help translating your emotional promise into platform content, or encouragement when the visibility work feels overwhelming, the support is tailored to what you need—not a predetermined program.

The work might involve refining your ME Factor until it's sharp enough to guide every decision you make. Building reader personas based on actual patterns in your reviews and comp title research. Optimizing your Amazon presence so the metadata works as hard as your writing does. Creating content systems that feel comfortable instead of exhausting. Or simply having someone who understands both the creative vulnerability and the business discipline required to build an author career—someone who can hold space for both.

If you're curious about what strategic partnership might look like for your specific situation, you can learn more at: storyimpactconsulting.com.

Regardless of the path you choose, this book has given you the foundation. The rest is execution—and that's something you're entirely capable of doing brilliantly on your own.

If you found value in these pages, please consider posting a short review on Amazon or Goodreads.

Your feedback is a meaningful way to advocate for the ideas shared in this book and helps us reach a wider audience.

Follow Lisa Towles at https://linktr.ee/authortowles.

www.ingramcontent.com/pod-product-compliance
Lightning Source LLC
Chambersburg PA
CBHW071550030726
47593CB00001BA/98